Hints To
Lady Travellers

At Home
And Abroad.

By
Lillias Campbell
Davidson.

First published 2011 by Elliott and Thompson Limited
27 John Street, London WC1N 2BX
www.eandtbooks.com

ISBN: 978-1-9040-2791-1

Material in this book originally published as
Hints to Lady Travellers: at home and abroad
by Lillias Campbell Davidson
London: Iliffe & Son, 1889

9 8 7 6 5 4 3 2 1

A CIP catalogue record for this book is available from the British Library.

Printed in Finland by Bookwell

Royal
Geographical
Society
with IBG

Advancing geography

Contents.

Home travel.

14 Accidents
18 Apartments
24 Baths
27 Boarding-houses
30 Booking-offices
33 Cabs
34 Cab fares
37 Cushions
40 Cycling tours
46 Dress
53 Dress-hampers
55 Driving tours
57 Etiquette of travelling
60 Etnas

62 Excursions
66 Fees
69 Fellow-travellers
72 Food
78 Foot warmers
80 Guards
82 Hand-bags
84 Holdalls
85 Hotels
88 Hot-water bags
90 Inns
93 Insurance
94 Invalid comforts
97 Lady's maids
99 Ladies carriages
100 Lamps

102 Literature
105 Luncheon baskets
106 Luggage
110 Medicine chests
113 Money
118 Mountain-climbing
124 Night journeys
126 Packing
131 Porters
134 Pullman cars
135 Railways
137 Railway keys
138 Riding tours
140 Sandwich-boxes
141 Sea-bathing
146 Soiled linen bags

147 Summer travelling
151 Stations
153 Tea
157 Tea-pots
158 Toilet requisites
160 Trunks
165 Unpacking
170 Waiting-rooms
172 Walking tours
176 Watering places
178 Winter travelling

Foreign travel.
182 Continental travel
190 Sea-voyages

Preface.

NOW-A-DAYS when a hundred women travel to one who ventured from the security of her own roof-tree in bygone days, some practical hints and advice upon the wide subject of wanderings abroad may be useful and welcome to those whose experiences are less varied than those of their sisters.

A thousand conveniences and comforts have sprung into existence to meet the need of their assistance. A thousand new conditions of life have arisen, forced into being by the demand.

It is to offer a few suggestions as to the adoption of such means as may render our journeyings more pleasant, more comfortable, and more conducive to health, profit, and enjoyment, that this little book has been compiled.

The advice which it contains is entirely founded upon practical experience and observation, and the writer has endeavoured, as much as lay in her power, to make her suggestions useful to women of all means and conditions.

'I want to do it because I want to do it. Women must try to do things as men have tried. When they fail, their failure must be a challenge to others.'

Amelia Earhart, American aviator, pioneer and traveller (1897–1937)

Introduction.

'IF, BY MY ENDEAVOURS, *I have in any way assisted my sisters in their wanderings, or encouraged a single woman to join the path of travellers by land or sea, I shall feel that I have achieved the object of my labours, and that my task has, indeed, not been in vain.'*

So concludes Lillias Campbell Davidson in the first edition of what for many women in the late Victorian era would have been a liberating reading experience: an instructional handbook for use beyond the domestic confines of the home. Written by a woman for women, *Hints for Lady Travellers at Home and Abroad* was first published in 1889, penned by a prolific authoress whose direct but intimate style would later translate itself into fictions such as *The Confessions of a Match-making Mother* and *Uncle Joshua's Heiress—who shall it be?*. As a commercial author, Campbell Davidson knew her audiences' taste and appetite for adventure well; she catered for the emerging market of independent middle- and upper-class women travellers with a diet of practical and at times opinionated and outspoken advice.

Distinct from personal travel accounts, such as those of Mary Kingsley and Isabella Bird, who had set contemporary high standards for travelogue-style writing, Campbell Davidson provided the first practical women's manual on the pleasures (and trials) of travel. Written from an exclusively female perspective, she reflected the growing emancipation of women during a period of extraordinary growth in the variety of forms of transport and opening up of routes and opportunities in Britain (and the wider world) to the moneyed classes.

Following publication of the first English edition of *Baedeker* (a guide to the Rhine, in 1861) travel in Europe was steadily democratised. With guide book in hand men—and women — were able to explore and orientate themselves in cities without necessarily having recourse to the expense or need for a local guide. Where a *Baedeker* provided art and historical background, *Hints for Lady Travellers* would provide the essentials, what Miss Eleanor Lavish in E. M. Forster's A Room with a View would find indispensable, even if she were to throw away her guidebook to experience the true spirit of Florence.

At her most practical, Campbell Davidson saw the need to provide information at a more mundane level. The availability of new methods of transportation such as the bicycle greatly accelerated the ability of women to travel without necessarily having a man at hand to effect financial and logistical arrangements. Around the time of the foundation of the Royal Geographical Society in 1830, the expansion and boom in railways throughout Great Britain enabled fast and efficient travel across the country, whilst by 1854, when Isabella Bird first ventured to sail the Atlantic on one of the twice-weekly steam ships serving the route, although still an adventurous experience for her, independent travel by women had been established.

However, both railway carriage and ocean liner provided cultural dilemmas for the lone female traveller, and Campbell Davidson did much to reflect the growing emancipation of the period, suggesting for example, that to travel first class, with one's maid in third class was simply impractical: a servant should only be taken if the intrepid traveller could 'defy convention' and upgrade the maid to share the first-class carriage instead.

The bicycle played an important role in the expansion of mobility for middle class women and in 1896, Campbell Davidson would follow up the success of *Hints* with the *Handbook for Lady Cyclists* which provided all of the necessary mechanical and technical information required.

In an age long before *Lonely Planet*, *Rough Guides* and travel websites, *Hints for Lady Travellers* provided sound advice and encouragement to women for whom the world of travel was still a wide and unexplored region, and before whom its perils and its discomforts loomed with a totally unnecessary dread. Campbell Davidson's following was secured by her combination of wisdom and good humour, some of which stands to this day, including her sage advice to never eat a railway ham sandwich.

Alasdair Macleod
Head of Collections, Royal Geographical Society with IBG

Home
Travel.

Accidents.

It seems somewhat ominous to begin a book of hints on travel with so disastrous a subject, but we must bear in mind the proverbial philosophy which tells us that 'accidents will happen', together with the more consolatory truth that 'forewarned is forearmed'.

There are perhaps, in proportion, no more risks in travelling than in any other situation of daily life, and it is undoubtedly true that modern invention and skill have greatly lessened all such risks to a minimum. It is well to be prepared for every contingency in life, and a few practical hints may not be amiss to the intending lady traveller.

First of all, it may be laid down as a universal rule that coolness and self-possession in the time of danger are not only the greatest safeguards against impending accident, but the best life-preservers when that accident has become an established fact. Fortunately, courage and calmness in the hour of peril are no longer rare feminine virtues in the present day, and even where they have not been bestowed by nature, they may very easily be acquired by cultivation and education. As a broad general principle, a woman's place in the moment of danger is to keep still and be ready for action.

It is so much an instinct with the stronger sex to protect and look after the weaker, that in all cases of the sort, if there is a man at the head of affairs, he had better be left to manage matters without the hampering interference of feminine physical weakness.

If there is no man, the woman will have to act for herself, but even then she will find it the best plan to keep still till the decisive moment arrives. In all cases of runaway carriages, tricycles, etc., the only plan is to stick to the ship, so to speak. Jumping is fatal; the only chance is to hold tight and watch for the moment of capsize. In case of accidents at sea, such as the foundering of a steamboat, etc., if it be at night, dress as rapidly and warmly as possible, and, whether by day or night, make your way at once on deck. If possible, secure any provisions which may be at hand, rather than even valuables; food may become worth many times its weight in gold. Look out at once for a life-belt, and if one can be secured, tie it about your waist, close under the arms—not lower down, or you may find yourself floating feet uppermost in the sea. If no lifebelt can be secured—and the supply is often shockingly inadequate—it is as well to provide oneself with any light wooden article that may be about. If a boat be not available, such impromptu life-buoy may save your life. Above all, don't hamper the movements of others who are working for your rescue, but obey orders as if you were under military rule.

In cases of railway accident, at the first warning of a crash or violent swaying of the train, put your feet instantly upon the opposite seat. Carriages, in a collision, 'telescope', and the seats are often driven together with great violence, imprisoning their occupants so that it is impossible to extricate them. Minor accidents often happen,

such as slipping on a step, trapping one's hand in the window or door, or cutting oneself with broken glass. In all such small casualties, as in the greater ones, a lady who has been through a St John Ambulance course, and derived practical information from it, may be of great service either to herself or her fellow-travellers, by applying first aid to the injured.

It is wise never to travel unprovided with a small flask of brandy and water, a tiny case of court-plaster, with scissors, and either strong smelling salts or sal-volatile.

Not an uncommon cause of accidents in railway travelling is the falling of heavy articles of luggage from the nets in the carriages, which, by the way, as is expressly stated in most trains, are meant only to contain the lighter articles of passengers' belongings. I know a lady who narrowly escaped a broken neck by her husband's portmanteau falling upon her head from the luggage-rack above, and I should advise all my lady readers to put their own weighty encumbrances under the seat, and to make sure that they are not seated beneath anyone else's ponderous possessions.

A single word in conclusion: Never anticipate accidents, though you prepare against them. I mean, don't feel convinced, every journey that you set out upon, that peril lurks in ambush in your path. Don't see collision in every jolt of the train, and scent shipwreck in each lurch of the steamer. Travelling under such circumstances will become neither an enjoyment nor a benefit, and you had better remain at home all your days with a fire-escape tied to your window and a burglar-alarm ready to your hand.

Banish all sense of danger and all anticipation of accidents, if you want really to derive joy and advantage from your travels.

*A*partments.

As a general rule, it is more satisfactory to engage furnished apartments in advance of one's arrival at a place. It is often possible to hear of well-recommended rooms through friends and acquaintances who can speak of their merits from personal experience; and this plan is, without question, the most likely to ensure comfort in one's temporary abode. After all, it is the landlady and her ménage which have quite as much to do with one's well-being and enjoyment as the mere externals of one's surroundings, and no matter how satisfactory the appearance of everything may be, it is quite impossible to judge from the mere outside look what degree of comfortable treatment will fall to one's share. The experience of others is at least some solid basis to go upon; and the inconvenience and annoyance of changing to other lodgings after one is once settled are so considerable that it is quite worth one's while to try and avoid it. So that, if possible, it is wisest to obtain recommendations to the rooms you require.

It is also possible, though, of course, less satisfactory, to write to the postmaster or stationmaster of the place where you intend going, enclosing a stamped envelope addressed to yourself, and asking him to favour you with a few addresses of lodgings which he can thoroughly recommend. I have found this to succeed in most cases, and have by this means obtained useful and valuable information.

The convenience is most immense of feeling as you journey towards your destination, perhaps hot, weary and dusty, or half perished with frost and cold, that your rooms are ready and waiting for you, with a meal prepared for your arrival, together with a well-aired bed and a fire, if it be winter.

Should it, however, be impossible to make any such pleasant and comfortable arrangements, it is as well to go at once for the night to an hotel, or so to arrange matters as to ensure one's arrival sufficiently early in the day at one's destination, to allow plenty of time for the selection of lodgings, as well as daylight, to choose them by. Rooms that look neat and attractive enough by gaslight may betray the guilt of dust and dirt by the unflattering glare of the sun; and one is too apt, late in the evening, to close with the first accommodation which comes to hand, with an 'any-port-in-a-storm' feeling, which one may afterwards live to deplore.

Always insist upon a personal inspection of each several room before you engage it, unless the recommendation be one upon which you can thoroughly depend. One can generally tell at a glance if the place be clean, if there be any objectionable outlooks, etc.

While in lodgings all valuables should be kept under lock and key, as well as any such articles of food as may be kept in the lodger's rooms. This is only a wise precaution, and by no means indicative of either a miserly or suspicious nature on the part of the owner.

Landladies may be perfectly honest, and should always be considered so till they prove themselves unworthy of the trust; so may their servants, *but the latter are, as a rule, drawn from a very inferior class, and it is neither right nor kind to expose them to a temptation which they may be unable to resist.*

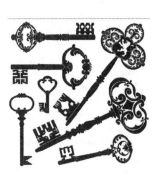

Keep your belongings under lock and key—in your own trunk, for preference, if you have jewellery or much money with you—since drawers and cupboard may possess duplicate keys.

Among the articles generally charged as 'extras' in the bill are fires—kitchen fire at all seasons, and other fires as you order them—lights, boot-cleaning, washing of bed and table linen, use of the cruet-stand (a curious item, this latter) and attendance.

It is so much a tradition of lodgings that toll is taken downstairs of the lodgers' food, that one is prepared to hear that 'There's nothing left, not a scrap, mum,' of the larger half of a fowl, or the goodly portion of pudding, when one requests its reappearance; and the lodging-house cat is a national joke. We all remember the paterfamilias in Punch who sets his artistic daughters to sketching the leg of mutton before its retirement downstairs; and I was once in a large and fashionable lodging-house where my serv-

ant betrayed to me the fact that the landlord's entire family subsisted on the bits annexed from the different dinners cooked in the house.

I have been in lodgings where every fragment of food I left was served up again and again with scrupulous fidelity, till I was sick of the very sight of it.

All damage to furniture or ornaments in the lodgings caused by a lodger during her stay, must, of course, be paid for by her, and it is just as well to take a careful look round on one's arrival, and to draw the landlady's attention to any visible damage as having been done beforehand. That this is not always an unnecessary precaution may be gathered from the fact that there actually exists a system among some lodging-house keepers of charging every fresh lodger for the same bit of damage.

I personally know of one bedroom carpet, stained by the overflow of a bath two years ago, which has since been charged to the account of, and paid for by, some ten or twelve consecutive occupants of that self-same room.

Damp sheets surely need no preaching against. Everyone knows their deadly effects, especially in this climate. Never get into a strange bed without being sure that it is well aired. The old-fashioned test of a hand-glass between the sheets is a simple one; and the faintest clouding of the glass is confirmation sure. If the slightest suspicion rests on the dryness of the bed, let that be its condemnation. Strip off the sheets, and sleep between the blankets—an unpleasant but a safe precaution. Dr. Jaeger's sleeping suits are admirable in such a case, and no lady traveller should be without them in the winter. They have certainly saved many a valuable life.

'ON THE FIRST day, at dinner, the mozo (waiter) perceiving that Anna had not regaled herself with a certain dish of calf's head, which he seemed to think very highly of, handed it to her, expatiating vastly on its merits of garlic; while, in endeavouring to make her comprehend the full force of its nature, he repeatedly touched his own forehead, with a leer, saying, "Cabeza de ternera, linda senorita, cabeza de ternera!" ("Calf's head, pretty senorita, calf's head!") which striking her as being a capital joke, to say the least, she was persuaded to try his calf's head, and see, if she could not taste, what it was made of.'

Anna Bishop,
from Travels of Anna Bishop in Mexico, 1849

Baths.

It is a great convenience to take one's own bath with one in travelling, since, although they are generally to be obtained in all frequented resorts at a slight weekly charge, as soon as one gets off the beaten track there is often great difficulty in providing oneself with this necessity of daily life.

In small country inns in the remoter districts of *Wales or the Highlands of Scotland it is sometimes next to impossible to obtain a decent tub, and the comfort of having one at hand among one's own luggage is very great.*

Travelling baths are very convenient receptacles for packing one's belongings into, as they hold a great deal, and the lid fastens with a strong strap and padlock. Needless to say, one should always be pretty well assured that the bath is perfectly dry and well wiped out inside before packing it with clothing, etc. A great addition has lately been made to travelling baths in the shape of a light wicker framework to fit inside, which may be lifted out bodily with its contents, thus obviating the bother of having to pack and unpack the bath every time it is used.

A supply of bath towels had better always form one of the contents of the travelling bath, since the towels generally supplied one in hotels and lodgings are remarkable neither for their quantity nor their quality. Soap and sponges should be added, that all bath necessaries may be at hand without the trouble of unpacking other boxes to hunt for them.

'**PROPOSING TO COUNT** how many different headgears are to be seen in Bombay alone, we had to abandon the task as impractical after a fortnight. Every caste, trade, guild, and sect, every one of the thousand sub-divisions of the social hierarchy, has its own bright turban, often sparkling with gold lace and precious stones, laid aside only in the case of mourning. But, as if to compensate this luxury even the members of the municipality, rich merchants, and Rai-Bahadurs, who have been created baronets by the Government, never wear any stockings, and leave their legs bare up to the knees. As for their dress, it chiefly consists of a kind of shapeless white shirt.'

Helena Petrovna Blavatsky,
from *The Caves and Jungles of Hindostan*, 1892

Boarding-houses.

The system of boarding-houses for people of the better class is one which has prevailed for many years in America, where, indeed, boarding-house life is reduced to a science, but has only been introduced into this country of comparatively late days.

Like all systems, there is much to be said both for and against it, and lady travellers must weigh for themselves the advantages and disadvantages which attend it. In its favour are the comfort and absence of trouble entailed by being provided for without bother on one's own part, and to very many women the idea of not having to cater for one's own wants, and to settle beforehand what one's dinner shall be, has a peculiar and irresistible charm which is all its own. Then, too, to a lonely woman there is the social aspect. One is surrounded by one's fellow-creatures instead of being cast 'friendless, solitary, slow' upon one's own resources in dreary rooms. One may make acquaintances, if one be so disposed, and the common interests of life under one roof draw people together.

One of the chief drawbacks to many women of retiring habits is the total lack of private life involved in the boarding-house system. One is cast from morning till night into a sort of spurious family circle composed of total strangers, among whom there will doubtless be always a pleasant element, but amongst whom, as in all gatherings of poor human nature, there are sure to be uncongenial or offensive people whom it is quite hopeless to think of avoiding. In one's own home, or in lodgings, one can flee from the annoying alien, but not so under the boarding-house roof. The public rooms are free to all, and you cannot even receive a friend in privacy unless you choose to entertain her in your bedroom. As to talking to her in a room filled with curious strangers, who can overhear and take mental notes of your conversation—the process is not exactly an inspiring one!

Boarding-houses are, as a rule, perfect hot-beds of gossip. It is perhaps only natural that a collection of total strangers, quite ignorant of each other's antecedents, thrown together in the intimacy of every-day family life, should take a particular interest in each other's affairs, and give the reins to curiosity and speculation.

There is apt to be a certain monotony in boarding-house bills of fare, and, if the establishment be conducted on economic principles, a tendency to serve up remnants, and curtail quantity. Then, too, it is very trying to some people, especially if they are blessed with delicate appetites, to be confined to a table d'hôte arrangement, without the privilege of consulting their own tastes.

As a study of life and character, there is perhaps no happy hunting-ground like a boarding-house, and the lady traveller who occupies the position of an observer of man and manners may derive considerable enlightenment and entertainment from her sojourn there.

Let me not be understood to mean that it is only the worse side of human nature which she will find exposed to her searching glance. I only mean to say that nothing brings out personal characteristics so much as life among strangers under one common roof, and though the student of her fellow-creatures may see much to excite her cynicism and her pity, she will also see in bold relief many of those qualities which excite her admiration and her respect, and acquaintances begun amid the common interests of the daily boarding-house routine may blossom into friendships which may endure for a lifetime.

Booking-offices.

The mind of the intelligent foreigner can never quite grasp the reason why ticket-offices in this enlightened country should be known by the above title. Of course it is a relic of the old coaching days, when places by the mail-coaches had to be booked beforehand in order to be secured. It is rather quaint, by the way, to trace the various survivals of coaching times which clung on, in this conservative nation, after the introduction of railways. For instance, the official in

charge of the train, instead of being a 'conductor' as he is in America, is still a guard, as in the days when he scrambled up and down at the back of the coach and performed wonders upon a post-horn.

The booking-office as at present constituted is not only a place for taking tickets, but an office for obtaining information of all sorts upon the subject of trains, etc. The booking-clerk is bound to look out trains, times, routes, etc., for all enquirers, and to answer all questions upon the subject. It is as well, however, to make all lengthy enquiries of this sort at some other time than the imminent departure of a train, while a crowd of wildly impatient passengers are trying to get served with tickets in their turn.

The very tiresome and unnecessary system which prevails of only opening the shutter of the booking-office a few minutes before the departure of a train favours a rush and scramble which is altogether uncalled for.

It considerably lessens the trouble, however, if travellers will observe the rules as to entering and leaving the little passage before the booking-office window, and will also facilitate matters if they have change ready to the exact amount of their ticket, and do not offer a sovereign to pay for nine-pence-half-penny worth of journey.

Conciseness in asking for one's ticket is also a virtue much appreciated by one's fellow-stragglers at the open window. 'One first, monthly return, Euston, please,' is likely to strike the listening ear of a waiter for his or her turn as a considerably superior effort of English to, 'I want to go to London—Euston Station, please. Will you kindly give me a first-class ticket? I should like a return ticket, a monthly return ticket if I can get one. You do issue monthly return tickets, don't you? I know they do by some of the lines. Or are return tickets on this line only available for a week?'

'FIRST, THE OFFICIAL says he does not like to take the responsibility of allowing me to endanger myself in those rapids. I explain I will not hold anyone responsible but myself, and I urge that a lady has been up before, a Mme. Quinee. He says "Yes, that is true, but Madame had with her a husband and many men whereas I am alone and have only eight Igalwas and not Adoomas, the proper crew for the rapids, and they are away up river now with the convoy." "True, oh King!" I answer, "but Madame Quinee went right up to Lestourville, whereas I only want to go sufficiently high up the rapids to get typical fish. And these Igalwas are great men at canoe work, and can go in a canoe anywhere that any mortal man can go"—this to cheer up my Igalwa interpreter—"and as for the husband, neither the Royal Geographical Society's lists, in their 'Hints to Travellers' nor Messrs. Silver, in their elaborate lists of articles necessary for a traveller in tropical climates, make mention of husbands.'"

Mary H. Kingsley, from Travels in West Africa, 1867

Cabs.

Extremely useful modes of transit to and from stations, though not always of the highest degree of comfort, especially in London. In the country, where they are generally known by the title of 'flies', one can often secure very comfortable specimens of degraded carriagehood, easy-going, though shabby, broughams, fallen from their high estate as private vehicles to minister to the wants of the general public. But the genuine old-fashioned London four-wheeler is a class of conveyance all to itself, and the very acme of discomfort, with its high, narrow seats, its rattling windows and broken springs, its generally musty and antiquated flavour. It is usually horsed with broken-down hacks which cannot be forced into anything like a pace, and for draughtiness in winter and stuffiness in hot weather, is altogether unequalled.

Cab fares.

It is as well to ascertain the amount of your fare beforehand, or you run considerable risk of being overcharged, cabbies, especially those in London, being exceedingly lax in their ideas as to charges, and generally making a point of demanding as much as they think there is any possibility of their getting.

They will often make the most preposterous charges with perfect audacity, especially when their victim is a lady travelling alone, and the younger and more easily deluded she looks, the better for their purposes.

It is just as well, when your porter calls your cab at the station, to ask him the fare to your destination, should you be ignorant of it yourself. Should he not be able to help you, the inspector or the policeman may do so; and though they are not always to be depended upon, still they form a certain ground of opinion on which to base one's resistance of exorbitant demands.

The safest plan, however, is to ascertain the distance beforehand, be sure that you are right, hand the cabman his exact fare (including charge for outside packages), and stick to it. The cabman may expostulate, or even become abusive, but the principle of not being cheated is a right one, and if you help to enforce it you are conferring public benefit.

The demand usually made by a cabman for 'something for himself' is one which has no legal foundation, and cannot possibly be claimed. Still, when one considers the wretched life of the ordinary cab-driver, and his inadequate pay, one is not inclined to grudge a small sop to Cerberus.

It is better, however, not to wait for the demand to be made, but to give one's offering the grace of a spontaneous effort, by adding a copper or two to the fare, with the remark that it is for himself. I always find cabmen very grateful for a stray newspaper, and often add the one I have just been reading to the coppers. I need hardly add that if there has been any attempt at overcharging the cabby goes without his honorarium and his paper. The kind-hearted but mistaken system which prevails at many houses in the country of giving the cabman who has brought travellers from the station a glass of beer or of spirits cannot be too strongly condemned.

Many a poor fellow has lost his place and his character from habits of intemperance begun in this way. If anything is offered, let it be a cup of hot tea or coffee, for which a cabman is generally most grateful.

The address to which you are going should always be given distinctly to the cabman, who, particularly in London, shows a wonderful cleverness in tracing out localities. Articles left or forgotten in a cab should always be at once applied for at Scotland Yard, if in London, or the nearest police station in the country, where, if the number of the cab can be given, there may be some slender chance of their recovery. The chance, however, is a very slender one indeed.

Cushions.

There is sometimes an innate hardness in the seats of country cabs, omnibuses, etc., and an inadaptability in the angles of railway carriages that can only be conquered by portable cushions and pillows. A new design of this sort has recently been introduced, known as the 'Melon', from its shape, which is very comfortable. But perhaps there is nothing more convenient than the ordinary indiarubber air cushion, which has the advantage of all others in point of portability, since, when emptied, it lies flat in an infinitesimal space, or will roll up into an ulster pocket, while a few seconds serves to convert it into a plump but yielding support.

These air cushions may, if preferred, be inserted in coverings of chintz or satin, which can easily be made to fit, and drawn over the not always artistic surfaces. A pillow of this sort will be found the greatest of comforts in a night, or long day journey, and will seldom fail to find its use as a supplement to the somewhat scantily endowed cushions of bed or sofa, when one is from home.

I am sometimes tempted to wonder what is the smallest allowance of feathers considered reasonable to supply with a hired room. I am certain I could readily have counted those in some of the pillows with which I have now and again been provided.

It may not be generally known that the jarring effect of a train or carriage, which some women find so trying and so injurious, may be prevented by the simple expedient of placing an air-cushion upon the floor under the feet. It is through the feet that the disagreeable jarring movement is communicated to the spine and the brain; and a journey will be found to be far less wearisome and exhausting in its effects if this plan is pursued.

For nervous invalids the addition of another cushion to sit upon is a still further prevention of headache and that shattering of the nerves which makes the mere thought of a journey by rail or carriage a nightmare to the imagination.

'WE WERE TIRED with our first day's ride, and as soon as we had spread our quilts, slept soundly for an hour or more, in spite of the noise and of the strangeness of our fellow lodgers, who after all, peasants as they were, had better manners than to interfere with us in any way, and who, when we woke up, let us have more than our share of the platform. Only there seemed no prospect of anything to eat beyond what we had brought with us. Everybody munched his bread as he did, apparently well satisfied with that for his evening meal. A little coffee was made and handed round, and about midnight the chuckle of a fowl announced that dinner was being thought of. But we were then long past caring, and in the land of dreaming again. A boy with the whooping-cough on one side of me, and the loud snoring of a muleteer were the last sounds I heard that night. Then the khan and all in it were still—all but the cats, which prowled about until morning, creeping stealthily round us and snuffing close to our face.'

Lady Annabella Isabella Blunt,
from Bedouin Tribes of the Euphrates, 1879

Cycling tours.

Tricycling has become so popular among women, and cycling tours such a feature of feminine travel, that a work of this sort would be incomplete without some reference to the subject. No style of touring is at once so enjoyable and so health-giving, and as more women experience the pleasures of the wheel, and the ease with which the possession of a three-wheeled machine will enable them to cover miles of ground in a most conveniently short space of time, there is little doubt that the cycling tourists of our own sex will soon equal those of the other.

It is a mistake to plan beforehand too long daily distances. The first day or two should be taken very moderately, and there should not be the least false shame about stopping to rest as often as one is tired, or at calling a halt altogether earlier than was at first intended.

Cycling for women has only two real perils—that of over-fatigue or of catching a chill when overheated; and these dangers may be reduced to a fraction by reasonable prudence and common-sense.

The first day of the tour the unaccustomed rider will probably feel somewhat tired and stiff. A hot bath and good night's rest will generally set matters right, and she will be surprised to find how the fatigue is lessened the following day, and so on, till the first ten or twelve miles which exhausted her are exchanged for the thirty or forty which only serve to raise her spirits and exhilarate her pulses.

It is a mistake ever to start on a tour on a machine to which one is not thoroughly well used, and a tricycle of one's own is fifty times better than a hired machine.

Tricycles are now made so light for ladies' riding that one can hardly believe in the labour involved in propelling one some six or seven years ago, and a good machine 'by a trustworthy maker' ought to be so strong and truly put together that there is little fear of misadventure from ordinary wear and tear.

Nevertheless, have your machine thoroughly overhauled by a good mechanic before you start touring. Nuts should be tightened, spokes tested, and a thorough cleaning should ensure easy running and unsoiled gowns.

The subject of dress is one

which requires a certain amount of careful consideration in cycling at all times, and in touring in particular. As little and as light clothing should be worn as is compatible with warmth—cycling is an exercise so violent that heavy or hot garments are totally out of place. Dr. Jaeger's sanitary woollen under-wear, or some of the English-made goods on the same system, are the best in winter, though thin merino will be found far more bearable in summer heat.

Wear as few petticoats as possible; dark woollen stockings in winter, and cotton in summer; shoes, never boots; and have your gown made neatly and plainly of C.T.C. flannel (not the cloth, which is too thick and heavy for a lady's wear), without ends or loose drapery to catch in your machine. It should be of ordinary walking length, and supplied with a close-fitting plain or Norfolk jacket to match. Grey is the best colour—dark grey. After that, perhaps, comes a heather mixture tweed, which does not show dust or mud stains, and yet cannot lose its colour under a hot sun.

If stays are worn at all, they should be short riding ones; but tight lacing and tricycle riding are deadly foes. All flowers, bright ribbons, feathers, etc., are in the worst possible taste, and should be entirely avoided. As for the hat, that must be a matter of individual taste and fancy, only stipulating that it should be neat, plain, and unlikely to be spoiled by exposure to wind and weather. Straw sailor hats supply the necessary shade to the eyes in summer, and a plain dark felt, not too large as to the brim, and trimmed with ribbon which will not spot with a dash of rain, forms a capital and suitable winter covering.

A mackintosh cape, one of the thinnest and lightest possible to procure, should always be carried to protect the shoulders in case of a sudden shower, and a fur cape for chilly evenings or east wind will be found a most comfortable addition. The danger of a chill following on overheating can, as I said before, be greatly reduced by simple precautions of this kind. A silk handkerchief to tie round the throat is also very useful, and can be folded flat, and stored away in the pocket of one's jacket.

Luggage is a vital question in cycle touring, the added weight of even a few pounds being a serious matter when one has to be one's own luggage-van, and considerable ingenuity has been exercised on reducing one's necessities of the road to their smallest extent.

One good-sized M.I.P. bag strapped to one's machine ought to carry all that will be required in a fortnight's tour, since the convenient parcels post renders it perfectly possible to arrange for changes of garments to meet one, and be sent home at various stopping places along the route.

Toilets and night necessaries—all of these reduced to the smallest size compatible with comfort—a tiny case of cottons, needles, etc., for occasional needful repairs, a map and road book, as well as some lighter literature for the evening hours, and a collection of such useful articles as court-plaster, glycerine, sal-volatile, brandy, Liebig's extract, etc., will still leave room for an extra gown of thin material and uncrushable quality.

Oil should always be carried; and be sure that your oilcan is filled and your tool-bag supplied with rag, winches, screw-hammer, spanner, etc., before you start. Each morning you should inspect your machine before starting, clean the parts where there is friction, and apply (sparingly) fresh oil.

Lamps must always be carried, and should be kept filled and trimmed. Matches should not be forgotten, if the filling and trimming are to avail anything.

So many ladies tour, either singly or in companies of two and three, now-a-days, that they no longer excite the attention and surprise which, not so very long ago, were their lot. It is seldom or never that they find themselves subjected to either rudeness or annoyance, even in the remoter country districts. Nevertheless, it is as well to bear in mind certain simple rules—to ride by day only, as far as may be possible, and to avoid lonely and unfrequented roads at untimely hours.

The rule of the road in cycling is the same as in riding or driving, and vehicles which obstruct the road before one are obliged to give way at the notice of one's bell, which should always be sounded when coming upon either foot passengers or conveyances from behind. Indeed, it is as well to keep up a continued ringing while passing through the streets of a town, or in turning sharp corners, since the noiseless approach of a tricycle renders it peculiarly startling to unprepared minds.

Tandem tricycles have come much into favour during the last year or two, and possess certain advantages for touring over the single machines. There is more sociability and companionship than is possible on separate mounts, and the united power thus acquired for driving the machine leaves less work to be done by both parties. A higher rate of speed may also be obtained,

though this is by no means a thing to be cared about in touring.

One word to my lady readers. If the sharer of your tandem be one of the other and stronger sex, don't, for the latter reason, throw all the work upon him. Not only is there a certain amount of unfairness in such a proceeding, but it has been known to produce the disastrous effects of a considerable falling off of keenness with regard to future trips of the sort.

Dress.

The days are, happily, now long past when the cherished tradition of Englishwomen, that one's oldest and worst garments possessed the most suitable characteristics for wear in travelling, excited the derision of foreign nations, and made the British female abroad an object of terror and avoidance to all beholders.

Now-a-days we have

come to recognise the fact that antique waterproofs, side-elastic boots, and mushroom hats tied up with huge veils of crude colours calculated to set one's teeth on edge, are not exactly necessities of travel, and that there is no reason, human or divine, why a woman should not be as tastefully and becomingly dressed while on her journeys as at her own fireside.

A gentlewoman's dress will always be simple and inconspicuous out of doors, and more especially amid the hard usage and inevitable grime of travel will striking colours and noticeable styles of cut be out of place, and therefore to be avoided.

But tailor gowns have set the fashion to all the feminine world of simplicity in mode and colour of outdoor costumes, and travelling dress may now be in the very height of style and fashion, and yet so quiet and plain as in nowise to smite the startled gaze of the beholder.

To begin with the initial subjects of dress—the underwear—there is no rule in this, as in all other cases, so good as that of the least amount of clothing with the greatest degree of warmth. It is now so generally acknowledged that for health reasons nothing is so excellent as the all-wool garments originally introduced into this country by Dr. Jaeger, that most of my readers have probably tested their merits for themselves, and need no advocacy of mine upon the matter.

The same conditions of manufacture have been applied to English-made goods, which have the great advantage of being supplied to the market at far cheaper rates, and no one need, therefore, be without these almost indispensable adjuncts to winter travel. For summer they are, of course, too warm to be suitable, but their place should always be taken by thin merino or India gauze, even that slender protection next the skin being necessary in the constant draughts, exposure to changes of weather, etc., to which travellers in this favoured clime are subject. The great drawback to the wear of all-wool garments when one is away from home is the care needed in their washing, and the ruinous results upon them of injudicious laundry work. Now, however, that they are becoming so universal, their management must be getting more generally understood by washwomen.

It is as well, in confiding them to the mercies of strange laundresses, to furnish with them the printed directions for their treatment, which are always supplied with them when they are bought. Should this precaution prove insufficient, it is as well to send the garments home to one's own laundry or washwoman by the convenient medium of the parcels post.

Boots are, as a rule, better wear for travelling than shoes, though the latter are sometimes to be preferred for comfort and coolness. There is much to be said in favour of both buttons and laces. The latter are the most durable, the former the most secure. When buttons are used the great drawback is the way in which they furnish a shining example of the innate perversity of inanimate objects, by flying off at the most inconvenient time and places, and generally turning up absent at the moment when boots or shoes are being donned in a frantic hurry.

A very useful little invention (American, if I am not mistaken) to prevent such

is abundant, and the boots disinclined to perform his labours more than once a day, it is sometimes a problem how to look respectable. This problem is best solved by a bottle of kid-reviver, peerless gloss, or some one of the excellent preparations for restoring polish and a tidy appearance to one's foot-wear.

agonising occurrences is the boot button fastener, by which buttons can be put on in a second or two so securely as to prevent all fear of casualty.

It is often a work of great trouble, in remote country districts, to get one's boots properly blackened; and, in cases where one's supply is not large, the mud or dust

In America, where blackened boots can seldom be had for love or money, unless you are prepared to 'shine 'em up' yourself, these substitutes for the blacking-pot and brushes form part of every lady's toilet arrangements.

Stockings, in theory, should always be woollen for travelling. But comfortable as this plan is in winter, it cannot be recommended for summer, when thread, silk, or cotton will be found far more agreeable. While on the subject of foot-covering, I may mention that boots lined with fleecy wool, or with washleather, are most comfortable for winter travelling, when it is often very difficult to keep the extremities warm.

White petticoats are quite unsuited to travel. Not only do they soil quickly, but they crush deplorably, and entail the carriage of a stock of clean ones quite beyond the bounds of convenience. Petticoats of pretty dark striped material are capital, and in very hot weather a petticoat of striped Oxford shirting is cool but durable. Silk petticoats are the warmest for winter wear, but if economy prevents this luxury, my readers will find

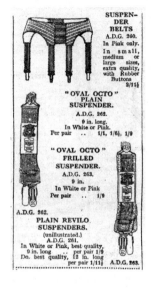

SUSPENDER BELTS
A.D.G. 260.
In Pink only.
In small, medium or large sizes, extra quality, with Rubber Buttons
2/11½

"OVAL OCTO" PLAIN SUSPENDER.
A.D.G. 262.
9 in. long.
In White or Pink.
Per pair .. 1/1, 1/6½, 1/9

"OVAL OCTO" FRILLED SUSPENDER.
A.D.G. 263.
9 in.
In White or Pink
Per pair .. 1/9

A.D.G. 262.

PLAIN REVILO SUSPENDERS.
(unillustrated.)
A.D.G. 261.
In White or Pink, best quality,
9 in. long .. per pair 1/9
Do. best quality, 12 in. long
per pair 1/11½

A.D.G. 263.

that an old silk skirt used to line even a thin stuff petticoat will impart a perfectly surprising degree of warmth.

As to gowns, nothing is so suitable as a plain tailor gown of either heather-mixture tweed, dark grey, or brown. For winter, tweed, serge or cloth may be used, and the lighter makes of the materials will be found useful all the year round. For really hot weather, a beige or good nun's veiling will be very comfortable. The make cannot be too plain.

The fastening of tailor gowns is usually simple and easy, and for a travelling dress this is a real point of comfort. To have to struggle into a gown of complex construction as the breakfast-bell is ringing, just with sufficient margin behind it to save the train, or as the boat is nearing its landing, is an experience calculated to make one look with a friendly eye upon the simple feminine toilets of the savage races.

Deerstalker caps are affected by many women in travelling, but suit very few, and where the effect is not exceedingly becoming it may be said to be very distinctly the reverse.

Hard felt hats are also good, especially when much change of weather may be looked for, as they do not damage nor lose shape as much as cloth hats in a thorough wetting. If a hat be worn in which it is uncomfortable to lean back in a railway carriage or coach, it is a good plan to carry with one a soft cloth hat or a knitted Tam-o'-Shanter cap, which will roll up into the pocket of one's ulster or travelling cloak, and which, on a long day's journey, will be found an unspeakable comfort.

A close, short lace veil is a great protection to the eyes from dust, wind and flying cinders, and in steamboat travelling is a boon in keeping the hair tidy and preventing in some degree the sunburn and freckling which is so apt to be produced by the glare of the sunlight on the water.

For summer travelling a dust-cloak will be found almost indispensable. These most useful garments should be made of linen or tussore silk, in any shade of grey, brown or tan. Even in the more costly material they are not expensive, and can readily be made by one's own maid or by oneself at home from a good pattern. They should reach to the hem of the gown, and be made to fasten all the way down if desired. They should be trimmed with yak lace to match the shade of material, and be relieved by knots of ribbon, either of the same colour or of some bright and pretty hue.

Dress-hampers.

Hardly any more convenient form of luggage than the dress-hamper or basket has ever been invented. It is large, yet light, waterproof, strong and durable, and an excellent harbour for gowns. Very excellent specimens of their class, with every improvement and in every variety, can be obtained of the best-known outfitters and trunkmakers throughout the kingdom for a few pounds. Of course, they are more suitable for dresses and the lighter articles of one's belongings, but they are also calculated to resist a considerable weight.

Even more cheaply may they be obtained in the following way, which I have proved from personal experience: I got a basket-maker to build me a strong dress-basket, the wickerwork close together like a basket, not open, as is generally the case with the framework of these articles. He fitted it with two light trays and a rounded top, added a strong, iron bar and padlock by way of fastening, and lined it throughout with waterproof cloth. It was one of the largest sized hampers of the kind, and cost me just eighteen shillings as it stood. I used it in this state for a year or two, then the corners began to get a little rubbed and broken, and I decided to have it covered. I sent it to a trunk-maker in a provincial town, who covered it for me with the strongest leather, fitted it with sole-leather corners, strong straps, etc., and assured me that it was far stronger and stouter than an ordinary open-work frame dress-hamper, and would last my lifetime. The end of that period I have not yet reached, so cannot corroborate his assertion, but certainly, after a very respectable amount of journeying, with hard wear and tear, and unsparing usage, it shows no signs of being one whit the worse, and I daresay it will outlast many of double its price, which it quite equals in every point of appearance.

No. G.G. 68.

Driving tours.

This is, like the cycle tour, a far more enjoyable and picturesque affair than the journey by train. It is, in fact, so replete with all the elements of entertainment and pleasure that one is tempted to wonder why it is not more frequently indulged in by people who could readily manage it.

There is a freedom in being able to choose one's own route and time, to hasten one's pace, or to dawdle through green lanes and lovely scenery, which forms a sort of fascination to the mind used to the conventional fetters of trains and time-tables; while the swift movement through the fresh air, and the ever-changing interest of one's surroundings, are things which fill the journey with a particular and an altogether inexpressible charm.

Here, as in other tours of the sort, it is as well to send on extra luggage, either by train or by parcels post, to meet one at certain points on the journey, and confine oneself to only what is absolutely indispensable en route.

In a driving tour in England, even in summer weather, one must observe the grand law of military life, 'In time of peace prepare for war'; and though one may be provided with a hooded phaeton, and supplied with indiarubber-lined rugs, etc., a driving rain or Scotch mist will spoil find out any weakness in the waterproof nature of one's personal coverings.

Mackintoshes are now so manufactured as to seem rather objects of beauty and adornment than the disfiguring wrappings they used to be.

A certain amount of provender for the horses must be carried on a driving tour, together with a few simple tools and appliances for remedying a breakdown should one occur en route. A field glass for distant scenery is a useful accompaniment, and sketching materials, or a pocket camera, can easily be stowed away with the other luggage, and will provide a constant source of enjoyment both during the trip and in after memories of it.

Etiquette of travelling.

There are certain unwritten laws which obtain in travelling, and which are as carefully observed by well-bred people as though they were the ordinary code of good society.

For instance, with regard to that fertile source of discomfort in railway travelling, open or closed windows, tradition has settled that it is the right of the individual seated nearest the window, notably the one who faces the engine, to decide the position of the pane of glass.

If a draught freezes, or close air threatens to suffocate the other passengers, they may politely beg the favour of an alteration, but they cannot insist; the matter is altogether in the hands of the corner seat person, and by his or her decision the others must abide.

So, also, with a seat whose owner has temporarily left it at a station, or which is engaged before the train starts. An umbrella, a bag — in fact, any article of the proprietor left there — secures it from appropriation by any other passenger, no matter how full the compartment may become.

At a hotel table d'hote, likewise, chairs tipped forward against the table are understood to reserve those seats against the invasion of all comers, and the claim is allowed and respected.

Punch has often held up to derision the British reserve and terror of liberties, which prevents the race at large from venturing to address their fellow-creatures before the correct form of an introduction has made them acquainted with each other. It is quite true that this is often carried to a perfectly grotesque extent, and people may travel in each other's society for hours, even days, without breaking through the gloomy and silent suspicion with which they regard each other. It is, however, quite as often due to ignorance of the world, and a lack of experience of other manners and customs than those of people's own land.

Persons who have been much abroad, and seen different men and manners, insensibly lose a great deal of this stiff unpleasantness of behaviour, and are ready at least to exchange the ordinary civilities of every-day life with those into whose society they are thrown.

There is certainly something very agreeable in the Continental habit of exchanging bows with every stranger who enters or leaves one's railway carriage, or hotel-coffee-room, and it grates a good deal on one's sense of human kindliness to return to the cold repellent stare, or the attempted unconsciousness, which replaces this habit of courtesy, in our own country.

True, it is part of the etiquette of travel that fellow-travellers, or neighbours at a table d'hote, may converse without having the magic formula gone through of a pronunciation of both their names—and that such an interchange of civilities does not necessarily constitute a future acquaintance—but a large portion of the travelling public prefer not to commit themselves even to this slight deviation from their usual customs, and remain as silent as the statue of Memnon in the latter days.

Etnas.

One of the most frequently felt wants in travelling is that of hot water, and it is a want which is by no means always as easy to satisfy as its simplicity would seem to promise. Especially at night is this often experienced, when kitchen fires are out, and no method of heating can readily be applied. Therefore, the so-called 'Etnas', or apparatus for quickly supplying boiling water, are most invaluable, and no lady traveller should be without one of these truly indispensable articles.

With a 'comfort' of this sort, either at home or abroad, one is altogether independent of extinct kitchen fires, or episodes of that domestic nature, and can be secure of providing oneself with boiling water at the shortest possible notice.

Methylated spirits must, of course, be carried as fuel, and it is as well to arm oneself with a sufficient quantity to last out one's travels, if possible, as it is very often difficult, once one is off the beaten track, to procure it in a pure and strong quality.

I shall never forget my trials in a remote town in Bavaria, where my stock of this needful article ran short, and I ransacked every shop in the place for a fresh supply, only to find all that I bought so diluted that it would scarcely even light, much less boil the water on which all my hopes of Englischez thé hung during my stay.

It is perhaps hardly necessary to warn my intelligent readers that lighted spirit must never be blown out, but extinguished by means of the little metal cap which covers the lamp, or else allowed to burn itself out. Many a fire has been the result of carelessness in this matter, and precaution will not be wasted.

Excursions.

The excursion is hardly a mode of travel to be recommended to the lady traveller, especially to the lady travelling alone. There is apt to be a great crowd, limited accommodation, and often much unpleasantness from a rough element. Nevertheless, it may often happen that the reduced fares of such an expedition tempt her to join, in which case she should be early at the point of departure, since the golden rule of the excursion system is, 'first come first served'.

Luggage is never allowed on day excursions, except such as may be carried in the hand, which, among the regular patrons of cheap excursions, consists mainly of plentiful provision for the way.

In the South of England, and in the agricultural

districts, excursionists are often of a mild and inoffensive type; but in the North, and more particularly in the vicinity of the large manufacturing towns, they are sometimes extremely objectionable in manners and conversation, and so rough that a gentlewoman will feel singularly out of place among them.

However, if she joins excursions, she must not take exception to her fellow 'trippers', and as an English crowd is almost always good-natured, even in its roughness, she will probably experience nothing worse than rough language and flashes of wit of a kind with which she is not upon terms of intimate acquaintanceship, and good-humoured toleration on her part will be decidedly the wisest policy.

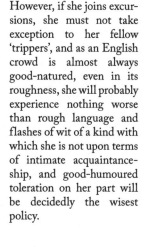

'WE FEMALE PASSENGERS thoroughly appreciated the stormless sea, and paced up and down the deck chatting and exchanging harmless confidences; the gentlemen tried to beguile the time with ring-toss and shovel-board. When they grew tired of such harmless occupations they got up a walking match, or ran half-mile races around the deck, and, indeed, in every way did their best to scare away ennui, and make the monotonous days and hours pass pleasantly; for after the first novelty of the scene is over, skies of eternal changeless blue and calm summer seas are apt to grow monotonous, and a thunderstorm or a howling hurricane, "warranted harmless", would have created a pleasant diversion. However, on the whole, time passed pleasantly enough; we were all sociably inclined, and lived on purely communistic principles, in a general exchange of civilities. Everybody was welcome to the belongings of everybody else; we used each other's chairs, rugs, wraps, and even made occasional walking sticks of one another's husbands, and when we had nothing else to do indulged in a game of speculation concerning the widow, who held herself aloof, in a state of as complete isolation as though she had been on a desert island; she accepted courtesies without a word of thanks, or refused them with an impatient gesture and died out, and as she resented any offer of assistance, she was left to stagger about the deck at her own pleasure.'

Lady Mary Anne Duffus Hardy,
from Through Cities and Prairie Lands, 1881

Fees.

A great nuisance in all affairs of life. This is getting to be more generally acknowledged, and the sensible step adopted by many public places of amusement, lines of steamers, etc., in abolishing fees, has been so greatly appreciated by their patrons that there is reasonable hope of a wide reform before long in this respect.

As a matter of fact, even where attendance is charged in a hotel or lodging bill, an extra special 'tip' is looked for by the waiter and chambermaid who have devoted themselves particularly to your service, and there are even cases when they have the audacity to demand what, from its very nature, is supposed to be a spontaneous offering.

The system of tips to servants in houses where one is a visitor is a particularly objectionable one, and though sanctioned by custom, is in the worst possible taste. The idea of paying your entertainer's servants for their attention to you while under their master's roof savours of the customs of an inn, and is indeed a falling off from the fine old national hospitality upon which we used to pride ourselves. If the guests are so many as to really cause great additional trouble to the servants, that fact should be taken into consideration in paying them their wages, and the expense should lie at the entertainer's door, not at that of his guest.

When one has really exacted an amount of attention from the servants beyond what may reasonably be expected, as in such a case as that of being ill at a friend's house, it is really nicer to offer a little gift rather than the coin of the realm.

Should that, however, be given, the fee to a housemaid may range from a shilling to half-a-crown, according to the length of the visit and purse of the visitor. To the lady's maid one may offer from half-a-crown to five shillings, but to those superior persons, the men-servants, one is expected to give gold if one gives at all.

At a hotel one tips the waiter who has attended one at table d'hote, or in one's private room. Also the head waiter, if one is so disposed, and has been long enough under that functionary's ken to have obtained any favours at his hands. The chambermaid who has your room in-charge will also expect to be remembered, as well as the Boots.

In lodgings you must fee the servants who have waited upon you (often most indifferently), and if you have hired the same carriage or Bath chair frequently during your stay, the driver will look for a small testimonial in the shape of silver coin when you leave.

At the sea-side the bathing-machine keepers who have charge of your bathing-dress must also be tipped; in fact, it seems a rule of travelling life that tips should flow in all directions at all times and seasons.

Tips to railway porters, though expressly forbidden by the byelaws of all companies, are so universally bestowed that the restriction has become a complete dead-letter. Conscientious scruples, it is true, prevent some people from depositing anything in the palm so instinctively extended when the luggage has been placed in the van and the seat secured in the carriage. But, after all, porters are an underpaid and overworked class, and almost invariably civil, attentive and obliging.

Fellow-travellers.

If boarding-house life brings out people's characteristics to a marked extent, the same may be said of travel of all kinds. Of all qualities which have a tendency to display themselves in people who travel, selfishness or the opposite virtue come out in perhaps the boldest relief.

It is really extraordinary to see the way in which people, well bred in all the other affairs of life, will fight for the best places, disregard each other's comfort, and evince a firm determination to consult no one's wishes but their own. Travel is certainly the true touchstone of character.

Much has been said about the danger to women, especially young women, travelling alone, of annoyance from impertinent or obtrusive attentions from travellers of the other sex. I can only say, that in any such case which has ever come within my personal knowledge or observation, the woman has had only herself to blame. I am quite sure that no man, however audacious, will, at all events if he be sober, venture to treat with undue familiarity or rudeness a woman, however young, who distinctly shows him by her dignity of manner and conduct that any such liberty will be an insult.

As a rule, women travelling alone receive far more consideration and kindness from men of all classes than under any other circumstances whatever, and the greater independence of women, which permits even young girls, in these days, to travel about entirely alone, unattended even by a maid,

has very rarely inconvenient consequences.

As fellow-passengers, perhaps, young babies are about as trying as any. Even the most devoted baby-lover must quail at the idea of a long dusty journey on a hot day, with both windows closed by an anxious mother to prevent possible draughts, and the sweet innocence of childhood displaying itself in robust roars which, like the brook, threaten to go on for ever.

A carriage specially devoted to babies and their guardians would be no bad thing, and may be suggested for the consideration of the different railway companies throughout the kingdom.

A little civility goes a long way in travelling. By the offer of books or newspapers, consultation of other people's wishes as to seats and open windows, generosity in sharing rugs, foot-warmers, etc., the wheels of one's journey may be oiled, and a pleasant feeling engendered, which will by no means be without result.

Real annoyance from fellow-travellers should never be endured. I mean such uncalled-for breaches of politeness as smoking in a carriage not dedicated to that pastime, where there are ladies, the use of bad language, quarrelling, or small indulgences of the sort. A remonstrance will very often have a good effect; but if that fails, the guard should be informed of the annoyance, and requested to settle matters.

In cases of real difficulty or danger, such as one of which I lately heard, when a lady found herself alone in a railway carriage with a lunatic suffering from violent homicidal mania, if the train is not likely to call a halt speedily, it is possible to stop it by means of either the cord of communication outside, or the newer arrangements, which can be reached from within.

Food.

Of all conditions in life, travelling is one of the most important times for carefulness and consideration in the matter of food. The great object should be to take as much nourishment as possible in the most concentrated form, and to avoid rich or unwholesome diet as much as in one lies.

Under all circumstances, the rapid change of scene, and the fatigue and over-turning of one's ordinary habits of life which travel-ling always brings about, to a certain extent, have a ten-dency to disorganise one's system, and care should be taken to obviate what may otherwise convert the joys and benefits of travel into a grave source of harm.

As a general rule, it is better to carry one's provisions, as far as may be, with one, or avail oneself of the refresh-ment baskets now to be had on most long lines.

The comfort of eating at one's leisure is only appreciated at its full value after a long experience of a struggle for places in a crowded refreshment room, followed by a hasty devouring of any eatable which presents itself to one's frenzied reach, and a watch upon the clock, whose hands fly over the dial face with an unearthly speed which suggests a confederacy with the agents who have contracted with you for a dinner at a fixed tariff.

This, however, is not always possible; and there is also a yearning on the part of poor human nature for hot food in cold weather, especially in the matter of breakfast, which can only be satisfied by an attack on the food department at a station.

Hot soup is, according to common sense and medical authority, the best and most sustaining form of food for travellers. Especially on a bitter day in winter is it grateful to the frozen voyager, though care must be taken that it is not served boiling on the arrival of the train. Yet one has heard such ghastly tales of station soup that many people shrink from the mere idea of it. In that case, a slice of meat from the joint, accompanied by potatoes, is perhaps the best substitute. Few vegetables should be indulged in, and little fruit—the latter never, unless perfectly fresh.

Avoid pastry as you would the plague, and confine yourself to plain puddings as far as may be.

Wine should be taken very sparingly, and spirits not at

all, except in case of illness. Hot coffee, tea, or cocoa will be found an excellent substitute.

Plain buns are really one of the most harmless styles of refreshment (though the spirit quails at the thought of the ordinary station bun, which resembles nothing in life so much as a geological fragment), or sandwiches may be eaten, provided they are not of ham.

After a long night journey, breakfast is an absolutely necessary consideration, and a really good meal should be taken, no matter what disinclination may be felt on the subject.

I know that a robust appetite is by no means a general characteristic of my sex, and everybody remembers the wit who once remarked that a woman's ideal of a solid meal was a cup of tea and a boiled egg, but I also am quite sure that it is the yielding to a feeble appetite, and leaving it to its own evil devices, which is the root of a vast amount of that 'little health of women' which is so universal a subject of wretchedness and unhappiness in modern life.

For travelling where much element of fatigue is introduced, and the portability of provisions is one of their chief requisites, such as walking and cycling tours, it will be found most useful to provide oneself with the extract of meat lozenges, which contain a really wonderful amount of nourishment in a most limited space.

Indeed, these are excellent things to accompany any journey, and will be found so easy a form of taking food as to be eagerly welcomed by most lady travellers. Some year or two ago one heard a great deal about coca—a preparation which was said to contain the greatest amount of strengthening and sustaining properties of any article yet discovered. A small cube or lozenge of this wonderful article was much recommended for the use of people who indulged in violent exercise, or were forced to journey long distances without food.

I tried these lozenges at the time, and found them so admirable that I should have no hesitation in recommending them to my lady readers, if I were, at the same time, able to tell them where they were to be procured.

When sandwiches are carried with one, great care should be taken to have them tempting both in taste and appearance. I have sometimes stayed at friends' houses where their cooks seemed far more accustomed to cut sandwiches for a men's shooting party than for a lady's luncheon, and I have found my sandwich-box filled, when I left, with thick chunks of bread and meat, so highly flavoured that I could scarcely eat them.

Delicately cut sandwiches are a temptation to appetite on a journey when a rough-edged crumbling layer of bread and meat would rob one of all desire for food.

Sandwiches of sardines, anchovies, pate de foie gras, or jam, though very nice at a picnic or an afternoon tea, are quite unsuited to travelling, as, though tasty, they are far too rich, and contain too little nourishment.

I have condemned ham sandwiches. This is on account of their thirst-inspiring qualities, and also because they are in no sense so good as those of tongue and chicken, beef, mutton, salmon or game.

It is best, in making long journeys, in which, under any circumstances, dust and heat combine with fatigue to produce a certain amount of thirst—it is best, as I say, to avoid taking anything which has a further tendency to produce this result. Sponge cakes, dry buns, sweets, etc., should all be carefully shunned; and a lit-

tle claret and water is better to take in one's flask than pure wine, which is apt to excite thirst.

Care should always be taken in throwing empty bottles, papers full of orange peel, etc., out of the window of a train to see that these rejected articles fall in a place where they can cause neither discomfort or inconvenience.

To throw out an empty soda-water bottle when the train is passing over a railway bridge above a crowded thoroughfare is nothing less than criminal, and the occupants of the rear carriages are often seriously annoyed by rubbish discarded by their fellow-travellers in the forepart of the train finding an entrance through their open windows.

When on a tour through an unfrequented part of the country, the food is often perforce plain and homely. One must not expect the finished cooking, nor the abundant supplies of hotel or home life, at rural inns, and one must be prepared to rough it somewhat, and be content if the necessities of life are supplied, without reference to the luxuries.

In these days of tinned provisions it is possible to carry about with one such luxurious additions to the ordinary bill of fare that these shortcomings of menage do not prove such serious inconveniences as they would have done a decade or two ago, and for any lengthy sojourn in remote districts, such as the mountains of Wales, the coast of Ireland, or the Highlands of Scotland, a supply of meat, fruit and vegetables, in those well-known round tins, will be found to be a real blessing.

A tin-opener should, however, not be forgotten among the equipment, as great inconvenience may arise from not being provided with this useful little instrument, which makes simple an apparently hopeless task.

It is just as well to furnish oneself on these occasions with one's own tea and coffee, which should be packed in air-tight tins. The decoctions supplied to one under the names of these useful and everyday articles are sometimes really too awful to describe, and the trouble of carrying about one's own supply will well repay itself.

Foot-warmers.

One of the greatest sources of discomfort and of danger to health in winter travelling is the affliction of cold feet. Railway carriages are, as a rule, regular draught-traps, and the lower part, exposed to a perfect current of air between two doors which seldom fit so tightly as to keep out all cold blasts, is generally of the temperature of an ice-house on a frosty day.

Foot-warmers are an immense comfort in these circumstances. They really act as heat-imparters to the whole person, since warm feet do more to quicken the circulation than half the people in the world seem aware of. They are supplied by all railway companies for at least the longer journeys, free of charge, during the winter months, though two very absurd arrangements may be noted with regard to them.

They are seldom, if ever, furnished to local trains,

though why people who are travelling for an hour or so by a way train are supposed to be less sensitive to cold than passengers by the express I have never been able distinctly to comprehend. Hot water is an inexpensive commodity, and even tins are not ruinous to provide in the first instance, and cost nothing to maintain. There is a peculiarly gruesome effect in leaving a hot foot-warmer in a carriage, whose temperature has been raised by its means, on an express train, and changing at a country junction into a way train, whose cold carriages, innocent of any means of heating, strike one when one enters with the effect of a family vault.

If one is travelling as, or with, an invalid, it is an excellent plan to provide oneself with a foot-warmer of one's own. They can be bought of tin or copper, with a green baize cover, and can be refilled as often as is necessary by the way. One of these will also be found very useful on a driving tour in early spring or late autumn.

Guards.

Peculiarly important functionaries on a railway. To them is entrusted the comfort, safety and well-being of all the passengers in the train, and to them must be referred all disputes, difficulties and vexed questions.

Ladies travelling alone are under the special protection of the guard, and, especially on the long-distance lines, are often placed, or place themselves, under his particular care.

To generalise on the species guard would, of course, be as impossible as to lay down hard and fast rules about any other section of mankind, but it may be stated as a broad principle that the railway guards in this country are almost invariably civil, attentive, and kindly to a perfectly superlatively degree.

Very different is the Continental official, espe-

cially in Germany, where the lady traveller, accustomed at home to find in the guard a respectful, obliging, and helpful assistant, is somewhat amazed to find herself rudely bawled at, her questions disregarded, and herself treated like a criminal under mild suspicion.

Of course, even in this country, one sometimes finds a railway guard who fails to sustain the character of his class. But the general rule makes the exception all the more marked.

'AS THE TRAVELLER who has once been from home is wiser than he who has never left his own doorstep, so a knowledge of one other culture should sharpen our ability to scrutinize more steadily, to appreciate more lovingly, our own.'

Margaret Mead

Hand-bags.

Under this denomination may be grouped all those smaller articles of the bag class which accompany the lady traveller on her journeys, and contain all her trifling needfuls for the way.

Courier bags (round leather bags with a strong lock, which may be slung over one shoulder by the leather strap affixed, and worn under the other arm) are very popular with ladies travelling upon the Continent, and, for extended tours in this coun-

try, may be found useful. They will hold one's money, note-book, etc., etc., and have the advantage of being safe, and not likely to be either lost or mislaid.

Waist bags are also a good deal affected by some ladies, and are perhaps even more secure and effective than the courier variety. These are made somewhat smaller in size, and lie very flat and compact. They are attached by two short leather straps to a strong leather waistband, and are perhaps one of the safest methods of carrying money in public that can be devised. They can be had from Messrs. Asprey & Sons, New Bond Street, and are somewhat more expensive than the courier bags.

The same firm have very neat little hand-bags, specially fitted up for ladies with writing and work materials. Those at £10 contain two scent bottles, with silver tops, and the following additional articles:

– An ivory hairbrush.
– An ivory clothesbrush.
– Ivory glove-stretchers.
– Ivory paper-knife.
– Tortoiseshell comb.
– Russia writing-case.
– Russia ink and match-boxes.
– Russia housewife fitted with good work instruments.

Empty hand-bags may also be had in every variety and at every price. If one is going on a short journey, these will be found most convenient, and are always of great use when one is away from home, in the way of taking out shopping, or on excursions, to carry one's purse, luncheon, book, work, etc. Those with a square frame and wide opening mouth are by far the best, as they hold more, and are far more convenient for filling.

A bag, to be really useful, should always be provided with a lock and key, in addition to the little snap catch which secures it. These locks are often not as strong or as easily worked as they might be, especially in the cheaper makes of bag, and this point should be carefully looked to in purchasing one.

Holdalls.

A number of loose wraps on a journey constitute a frightful nuisance; and one is often filled with compassion at the spectacle of an unfortunate lady struggling with an armful of rugs, fur cloaks, small knitted shawls, etc., etc., which threaten at every moment to escape her grasp.

Under these circumstances some article or another is pretty certain to be forgotten in cab or railway carriage; and the bother of keeping in mind the number of the varied assortment one has to collect when one reaches one's journey's end is itself a real affliction. As a remedy for this nuisance I may highly recommend the so-called holdalls, for rugs, sticks, etc. A variety of this article may be had to contain sticks and umbrellas alone (see umbrella cases), but for a miscellaneous collection of travelling articles, the holdall is by far the most convenient. It is a flat piece of waterproof canvas, sometimes covered with a fancy tweed, for greater elegance of appearance, which is rolled round one's rugs and smaller wraps, and secured by stout leather straps, forming a compact and neat bundle.

Hotels.

Perhaps there is no more comfortable method of living during one's absence from home than in an hotel. The relief from housekeeping bothers, or troubling over the ordering of dinner, and the supplying of provisions, is as great as in a boarding-house while there is far more freedom and independence than can be obtained in that system of pretended family life. Of course, in the long run, it is more expensive than any other style of living, but for a day, or two, or, indeed, even longer, it can be arranged with considerable economy if one knows how to manage.

The best hotels, which have a fashionable name, and keep up a certain expensive display, are, of course, far more costly than those whose situation may be less imposing, and their name less known. It is also by no means the case that gorgeous buildings and an array of gilding necessarily imply comfort in the arrangements. On the contrary, some of the old-fashioned so-called 'family' or 'private' hotels are by far more replete with solid comfort and convenience than some of the splendidly decorated and furnished 'Grands', 'Imperials', or 'Universals'.

An inferior hotel is not always a cheap one. One may find bad cooking, wretched beds, and miserable attendance, and yet be charged exorbitantly for them.

If one is young and nimble, and content to mount many stairs; or if one does not object to a view of a stable-yard, or a blank wall, one may generally obtain a bedroom at a good deal lower price. As the public rooms are free to all, and as one does not, as a rule, go to an hotel to pass most of one's time in one's sleeping apartment, such drawbacks in the accommodation need not be regarded as serious.

It is better to lock your door on the inside at night, even if you are not in the habit of doing so in ordinary life. The key should never, however, be withdrawn, as, in case of illness, an outbreak of fire, or any other night alarm, one should be able to undo the fastening in the space of a second.

All valuables, such as jewellery, extra money, etc., should be deposited in the manager's care as soon as you arrive. Otherwise, no one is responsible for them but yourself, or can be blamed in event of their loss; since, in a public place like an hotel, people are so constantly coming and going that it is impossible to trace the loss of one's possessions, or lay suspicion in any special quarter.

At many hotels in places of fashionable resort, it is usual, during the season, to give entertainments to the visitors—dances, or 'hops' as they are called, amateur concerts, etc. Hotel life under these circumstances may become very agreeable, and one often meets with pleasant people who help to make one's stay enjoyable.

Dress, in hotel life, is pretty much according to the taste and fancy of the individual woman. You are not remarked if you live altogether in your travelling gown, neither are you commented on if you change your costume seven times a day. At most hotels, however, there is a slight attempt, at least, to make some lightening of attire for the evening, and a plain black lace or net dinner dress will be found *very useful wear, since it marks the effort to 'dress' without erring on the side of being over gay.*

Some women appear to think that they have conceded sufficient to the prejudices of society as regards evening dress, if they add to their everyday costume a lace jabot, or an arrangement of India muslin and ribbons, which covers the front of their bodies. It is true that this simple expedient has a wonderful effect in lightening up a dark or sombre-looking gown, and in imparting a 'dressy' effect, but when it is applied to a heavy stuff gown, plain in texture and make in all other parts, the result is so incongruous as to be almost painful. Better far the honest unadornment of the travelling gown than such an inappropriate decoration as this.

Hot-water bags.

One of the most useful, I had almost said indispensable, accessories to travel. In winter there is nothing more comfortable, or, indeed, safer than one of these handy little articles to put into a cold bed, or one that is not altogether above suspicion in point of damp.

Cold feet are one of the chief causes of uneasy rest and sleeplessness, and are *more frequently produced by travelling, perhaps, than in any other way.*

Sometimes one may lie for hours without being able to get one's feet warm, if one has gone to bed with them thoroughly chilled, and there is nothing pleasanter, when wearied out by a long, cold day's travel, than to get into a bed well warmed by a hot-water bag.

In cases of illness they are also invaluable. They are so light and yielding that they may be applied to any part of the patient's body, and are most efficacious in cases of violent pain, inflammation, the first twinges of rheumatism, etc. They are so portable that they can be carried everywhere with one, either packed flat among one's clothes, or rolled up in the pocket of one's holdall with the rugs and wraps.

As for hot water to fill the bag, that is a commodity readily obtained almost anywhere on one's travels. Even where this is not the case, or where the time is inconvenient—such as the middle of the night—the lady traveller who is provided with her etna or her home comfort is quite independent of exterior aids.

She can boil her kettle in a few minutes, and supply herself with a hot-water bag in far less time than it would probably be procured for her by the servants at an hotel or in lodgings, and she will also be certain that it was filled with hot water, a point upon which the minds of most servants seem to possess a delicious vagueness.

Inns.

These comfortable institutions of our grandparents have now, alas! been almost merged in the noisy and vast hotel, and when one reads the fascinating descriptions of inn-life in some of Dickens's tales, or the stories of the last century, one is tempted sometimes to wonder whether one has altogether been a gainer in this respect by the march of civilisation.

True, we have gained in luxury and splendour, but we have also lost a good deal in solid comfort; and as for the friendly welcome, and the homelike feeling dwelt on so fondly by writers of a past day, one is tempted to smile at the idea of the contrast with a modern fashionable hotel, where one comes and goes almost unheeded among the jostling crowd, and where there is about as much feeling of home as might be experienced in an Eastern mosque.

Nevertheless, in various remote country districts, where the horde of tourists seldom penetrates, and the fashionable world never comes, there may still be found lingering a few survivors of the old condition, which open wide the hospitable portals of their wide coach yards, and entertain their guests with the dim and faded glories of oak-panelled staircase and four-post bed.

There is an old-world flavour about a hostelry of this sort that has its own peculiar charm; and something of the atmosphere of the long past days seems still to linger in the landlady's pleasant hope that we have slept well, and mine host's genial study of our personal comforts. There is still a lingering flavour of lavender about the sheets—sometimes of fine old linen, and very dignified, though chilly—and the cellar generally holds some famous old wine, though the stock has grown extremely scanty.

It is enough, under these circumstances, if the place boast of the virtue which is only secondary to godliness; and the food be all that could be desired in point of quantity without too great a strictness in the matter of quality. It is not, however, always the case that the charges are in an exact scale with the fare provided, and one is often a good deal surprised at receiving a bill which would not disgrace a first-class hotel.

It must be remembered that in these remote districts provisions are scanty and very dear. The actual necessities of life—bread, meat (mutton, that is to say—beef is often an unattainable luxury), etc.—are cheap; but everything beyond this has to be procured from the centres of civilisation, and the difficulty of carriage of course lends its aid in increasing the cost of procuring.

On the whole, however, to one who is not too spoilt by the over-luxurious living of our own days to enjoy the pleasures of a simple and healthy life, there is a degree of enjoyment for a little while even in 'roughing it' in a remote country inn.

Insurance.

There is an easy system of insurance against railway accidents whereby any traveller in taking a ticket at the booking-office can be further supplied, at a cost of a penny or two, with a ticket which entitles them in case of accident to claim damages.

These tickets, in case of death from accident, being found upon the body of the lawful possessor, entitle their heirs to claim a large sum of money from the insurance company.

There are also excellent accident insurance companies in which by the payment of a small annual sum disablement from accidents of almost any kind entitle one to a compensation. There is a special section for insurance against railway accidents, and the precaution for anyone who travels much is a simple and sensible one.

Invalid comforts.

It is wonderful under how much inconvenience and bodily discomfort an invalid is often forced to travel, when a little knowledge of ways and means would smooth away most of the difficulties.

Railway travelling, to anyone not in robust health, is attended at any time with much fatigue and unpleasantness, and these, of course, are much increased in the case of a regular invalid; but it is possible to greatly reduce the discomforts and inconveniences by a little thought and trouble beforehand.

For those to whom expense is no object, the invalid carriage is an excellent institution. It is far less costly, indeed, than is often supposed, being supplied by most railway companies at the price of three first-class fares.

These invalid carriages are furnished with comfortable couches, easy springs, abundant conveniences; and have the great advantages that they secure absolute privacy, and that they do away with the trying changes from one train to another, since the whole carriage is simply uncoupled from one engine, shunted to another line, and taken up by the new train.

Next, in point of comfort, is a first-class carriage, where the arms of the seats turn up, forming a comfortable couch along one side. The carriage can generally be secured for an invalid's use by favour of the guard; and a 'tip' on such an occasion is well administered. Even the side of a second-class carriage can be made very comfortable with rugs, cushions, etc.

Third-class carriages are often blessed with such narrow seats on the South of England lines, where reform is somewhat halting, that no amount of accessories can transform them into luxurious resting-places; but on the long-distance trains in the North, they are calculated for the use of people brought up in nineteenth century tastes and habits.

In many of the large stations, especially on the lines most frequented by invalid travellers, it is customary to keep a wheeled chair, or else a hand chair, with short poles, after the manner of a sedan without its outer case, to convey people who are unable to walk from one platform to another. Where these are not obtainable, it is as well to ask two porters to bring a chair from the waiting-room, and hold it close to the carriage door to receive the invalid—carriage steps being often one of the chief difficulties. Upon this improvised invalid chair the passenger can be lifted by her porters—porters are, happily, a stalwart race of men—and carried to the place of destination.

Food has often to be taken at regular intervals, and for this purpose Brand's meat jellies will be found most valuable. A small basket should be prepared, with all that is required for the invalid on the journey, that it may be at hand at a moment's notice.

If medicine is to be administered, it is as well to be supplied with a measuring-glass, graduated to all dimensions, from drops to spoonful. It is often a work of great difficulty to measure by spoon or by drop when one is in active motion in a train or boat, and an exact dose is always a matter of grave importance.

Brandy, sal-volatile, and strong smelling-salts should always be at hand in case of need. In summer a fold-up fan and a flask of eau-de-Cologne or toilet vinegar will be found a great refreshment, and an unlimited stock of clean pocket-handkerchiefs is almost indispensable.

In the case of invalid travel, common humanity generally abolishes all the usual rules of etiquette, and the invalid's convenience and wishes are supposed to settle all arrangements of ventilation, choice of seat, etc.

Lady's maids.

A great nuisance, as a rule, in travelling. Now and then one lights upon a brilliant exception, who looks after one's luggage and one's personal comforts, and takes one's tickets and the care of one's belongings in a way which allows one to dismiss all care from one's mind.

The majority of lady's maids are weak and impotent things in travelling. Of a class for whom

all arrangement are made, and who are accustomed to being managed for in every way, they are generally helpless in the moment of action, and worse than useless in an emergency.

The lady's maid is supposed to have the care of her mistress's dressing-case or bag in travelling, and to be responsible for its safety. She should also take the tickets, fee the various persons to whom such gratuities are due, see that the luggage is labelled, and settle her mistress in her carriage before seeking her own. The ideal maid is at the door of the carriage the moment the train stops, ready to take her mistress's wraps, and to assist her to alight, before looking out the luggage. In point of fact, in nine cases out of ten, the mistress has to do all the work herself, with the additional trouble of a feather-headed domestic to take care of.

The maid is supposed to travel second-class, or, in cases where the line boasts no accommodation of that exact grade, third. For a lady travelling alone, it is a far more sensible plan to take her maid into the same carriage as herself, where she can be of some use, and where her mistress is not haunted with the suspicion that she and the dressing-case may both be missing at the journey's end.

Ladies who travel in the less-imposing classes of carriages will bear me out in my observation that the most unpleasant fellow-travellers, as a rule, one ever is brought in contact with, are lady's maids and footmen. When several of this class get together their conversation is often characterised by a freedom and a laxity which would perhaps somewhat startle the mistresses whose private matters and tempers they are openly and loudly discussing.

Ladies' carriages.

Upon most of the long-distance lines there are to be found carriages specially reserved for the use of ladies travelling alone, of which, however, one often hesitates to avail oneself. The occupants are seldom of an order to invite one's longings to have them as fellow-passengers, and consist, as a general rule, according to my experience, of babies-in-arms with their natural guardians, and of aggressive-looking females, who certainly do not strike the beholder as in any way needing the sheltering shield of a carriage specially dedicated to unprotected females.

Lamps.

As a rule, lamps in railway carriages do not afford a sufficiently strong light by which to read or work with comfort. It is as well, therefore, for long distance or night journeys to carry with one a portable reading-lamp, which will be found a great comfort and convenience.

The most convenient arrangement I have ever tried, however, was a little electro-silver reading-lamp lent me a year or two ago by a friend when I was travelling to the Scotch Highlands, and had a long night journey from town. It consisted simply of a case to hold the candle—which it exactly fitted—with a strong, self-acting spring, which raised the candle to the proper height as fast as it burnt down.

I have never seen another lamp like it, before or since, and apparently the general public shared my experience, for I remember the small crowd which gathered round the window at Euston Station to gaze upon my little arrangement with the most intense interest and curiosity.

Literature.

Travellers, now-a-days, are pretty abundantly provided with material for reading on their travels; and a glance over Messrs. Smiths' book-stalls, in any of the railway stations or on the pier heads, would make one fancy that the taste which could not find its own particular food amongst that varied assortment must indeed be hard to please.

The railway-novel, that particularly modern style of book, has even been called into being simply to beguile the traveller's idle hour; and consists of a quality of literary work too flimsy to serve any other purpose than that for which it was meant.

To some people, reading, while travelling, is an abhorrent thing, either because of the strain to the eyes (this, in railway journeys, is really a serious thing, and is supposed by some people to be one reason of the short sight so common to the present generation), or because they prefer looking at the scenery. Another class of persons, on the contrary, may be discovered on the top of an Isle of Wight coach, or on board a steamer among the Scotch lakes, so buried in a volume of the yellow-backed species as to be oblivious of the entire world about them.

As a rule, deep or profound reading is not suited to the requirements of travel, and may well be kept till one has settled down to a sufficiently protracted stay to make it possible to steady one's mind to grasp it. All the world does not appear to share this opinion, since I once travelled in company with a young Scotchman, on his way home from a German University, who had provided himself with four stout volumes of the Ethics of Aristotle, apparently as light mental refreshment for the journey.

It is perhaps as well to select beforehand the books, magazines, or papers which are to beguile one's moments of travel, and not to trust to the hasty choice in the station at the last moment; since, under the latter circumstances, one may often find oneself in the possession of something so absolutely imbecile that not even the conditions of travel can reduce one to reading it.

In connection with literature one must not omit to mention the vast class of books and periodicals which have travelling and travellers for their chief subject.

Under this head may be classed all the guide-books, books of travel, etc., which increase yearly, and which form a perfect library of themselves. Of the number of guide-books, Black's guides to the various parts of the United Kingdom may be reckoned as complete and accurate as any. A capital little book called 'All About Our Railways' has lately been published, and may be had at all the railway stations.

A little magazine called 'The Tourist and Traveller', and, as its title suggests, catering for travellers with varied information on the subjects of 'hotels, railways, steamships, holiday-makers and pleasure-seekers at home and abroad', can be highly recommended to the notice of my readers.

Luncheon baskets.

At the principal stations on the long-distance lines Messrs. Spiers and Pond have a system of providing luncheon baskets provisioned for the use of the passengers. These baskets are carried to the trains by boys, and can be obtained at various prices, according to size and contents. They hold provision for a meal, together with the proper accompaniments of plates, knives and forks, etc.

Private luncheon baskets are also very good arrangements in cases of long journeys, and may be carried out at considerably less cost than a continued course of those supplied by the refreshment rooms.

Messrs. Asprey & Sons have some which are most compact and capitally fitted up, in sizes varied for the accommodation of from one person to twelve. Those for one traveller are fitted with the following accessories:—

– A porcelain dish
  and metal top.
– A wicker-covered bottle with a screw top.
– A tumbler with a
  wicker cover.
– One enamelled plate.
– Plated fork.
– Ivory-handled knife
  with plated blade.

Luggage.

'If it were not for its pleasures,' said the cynic, 'life would be endurable.' Let us parody this remark, and say that if it were not for its luggage travelling would be a purer joy. One is inclined to envy the artless sons of toil, with their knotted red handkerchiefs hung at the end of a knotted stick, and containing all their wardrobe.

From first to last luggage is a terrible bother, and must remain so till the present conditions of travel in this country are modelled more after the American plan. There the nuisance is greatly abated, and, in fact, almost removed. One simply sends to the nearest express office (a sort of enlarged Carter Paterson), and an express waggon calls round in due course, and collects your boxes. To each of them is affixed a round brass label, or 'check', bearing a number.

Duplicate checks are handed to the owner, and the luggage then vanishes. Down goes the traveller to the train, takes her ticket with no fuss of porters, labelling, etc., etc.; and with a mind at ease, and filled with tranquillity, arrives at her destination.

Perhaps half-an-hour after she has reached the address, which was attached to her boxes, has got her greetings over, and is settling down in her new place, comes the express waggon with her luggage.

She shows her checks, and the boxes bearing the corresponding numbers are delivered up. Certainly it is a system which compares favourably with our own, in the saving of worry and trouble, and avoiding of anxious thought.

Luggage, in this country, is a source of carefulness from the moment it is bumped up on the roof of the cab which is to convey one to the station, to the time when one sees it deposited at its destination. If one does not personally see it labelled, the railway companies disclaim all responsibility in connection with it; and even then one is not secure from peril as regards it.

Be particular, therefore, in the first place, to see that your luggage is plainly addressed; and in the second, that it is properly labelled. After this, watch it till it is deposited in the luggage-van, and remember the position of that van in the train.

Arrived at your destination, or, being forced to change at a station, tell your porter the van where your luggage is placed; the number of your packages, and the place from which they came. This will facilitate matters in finding it.

If you stand near at hand while the luggage is being removed from the van, you will be able at once to point out your own special belongings. People who have travelled much abroad generally adopt the plan of having some special design painted on the sides or ends of their luggage—such as a bar, a circle, or a cross, in bright colour. This forms a distinguishing mark, like the brand of a sheep, and enables them to identify their own boxes at a glance. It is a plan possessing great advantages.

There is a settled allowance of weight for passengers' luggage by each class, and if your belongings exceed their standard they are charged accordingly. Now that so many more ladies travel second and third class than was formerly the case, this rule is sometimes a great inconvenience; though it is seldom rigidly enforced, unless the luggage is really greatly in excess. If the over-charge is very great, it is sometimes worth one's while to travel by a superior class, where the allowance is greater; but this must be ascertained beforehand, since the luggage is not weighed till after one's ticket is taken.

'AT THE COMMENCEMENT, I found my journey quite intolerable, as I could never sleep travelling. Hence it may be imagined that my weariness was extreme, and that a few hours' rest had become absolutely necessary to recruit my failing strength. After travelling for two days and nights, on arriving at a station for the relay of horses, I alighted from the sledge and entered the post-house. Completely exhausted, I sank on the nearest bench, hoping to procure some repose, though it were only for one short hour. But from the agony of my mind, all my endeavours to snatch a little sleep proved ineffectual, for although my body was, from sleeplessness, in a wretched state of prostration, my mind, to my great distress, continued all the while active, and kept me awake.'

Eve Felinska, from Revelations of Siberia, 1853

Medicine chests.

It is well to be provided, in travelling, with a few simple medicines for use in case of sudden need. Indeed, one may be placed in a position where chemists' shops are as unattainable as the philosopher's stone, and there is actual risk of danger to life if one has not some provision of a medicinal nature about one.

I well remember spending the autumn at a Highland shooting in the wilds of Sutherlandshire, where the nearest doctor was sixteen miles away; and, when sudden and serious illness occurred one night in the house, the whole resources of the household were found to be confined to a packet of mustard-leaves and a bottle of antibilious pills!

It is safer not to run the risk of being placed in such a predicament as this, and on this account I strongly recommend every lady traveller to be her own chemist for the time being.

Messrs. Silver & Co. supply capital little medicine chests, in solid leather or oak, fitted with bottles, scales, measure, knife, etc. They are exceeding compact and handy.

These little chests are fitted with strong locks and keys, and should be invariably kept locked if they are left about.

Even perfectly harmless drugs should never be exposed to public curiosity and ignorance. Lodging-house and other servants have often a perfect craze for tasting anything which is novel to their experience.

I once knew a lady whose maid nearly died from having eaten the greater part of the contents of a box of Tamar Indien [used for biliousness and constipation, among other things], which she found upon her mistress's dressing-table, and mistook for a new-fashioned sort of bon-bon!

One can either have one's medicine chest filled by a chemist, or supply it oneself, according to one's own personal needs and liking.

All or some of the following list of articles will be found most useful:—

- Lamplough's Pyretic Saline.
- Eno's Fruit Salt.
- Quinine Pills.
- Vaseline.
- Cockle's Pills.
- Holloway's Pills.
- Holloway's Ointment.
- Dover's Powder Pills.
- Colocynth and Colchium Pills.
- Pepsine Pills.
- Camphor Pills.

- Seidlitz Powders.
- Glycerine.
- Insect Powder.
- Sal Volatile.
- Methylated Spirits.
- Sanitas.
- Tamar Indien.
- Eau de Cologne.
- Friar's Balsam.
- Chlorodyne.
- Tincture of Arnica.
- Essence of Camphor.
- Oiled Silk.
- Mustard Leaves.
- Cough Lozenges.
- Court Plaster.
- Caustic.

Those ladies who patronise homœopathy are more fortunate than their fellow-women, since their minute bottles of pilules and tinctures pack in even more compact and portable cases.

Money.

There is always a good deal of anxiety connected with money in travelling. Ladies, as a rule, are not so conveniently supplied with the means of carrying this necessary but troublesome commodity as are the members of the other sex; and a purse is a thing which is easily lost, mislaid, or stolen.

It is unwise to carry large sums of money about with one, and it is safer only to put in one's purse such an amount as will be required during the day's journey, with a margin over for unforeseen occurrences, possible loss of ticket, etc., etc.

Surplus gold and notes should be sewn into the bodies of one's dress, or in some such secure place of refuge. Many ladies put theirs in the drawer of their dressing-case, or some such ordinary receptacle; but as a dressing-case is always supposed to contain valuables it is much more likely to be carried off bodily, spare cash and all, than any other part of one's belongings. Neither is it safe to put much money in one's boxes, where it is exposed to perils of various sorts.

It would be wiser to leave most of one's money at home, and trust to one's cheque-book while on one's travels, were one always sure of being within easy reach of a bank. Indeed, even then, it is most difficult to get a cheque for any considerable amount cashed at a bank where one is not known.

Five and ten pound notes are better in such a case, and can always be paid into a bank, but they are more likely to be stolen; and are very difficult to pass in the country districts, where the tradespeople may object to take them unless they know you. Numbers of bank-notes should always be taken, that the payment may be stopped in case they are lost or stolen.

Perhaps as good a plan as any is to convert five or ten pounds into postal orders, made out to oneself. If they are then signed with one's name, they are pretty safe, and the name of the post-office can always be filled in as occasion requires. These postal orders have the portability of bank-notes, and are safer; besides being readily changed in districts where there are no banks to visit.

In Scotland the one pound notes are a convenience, and in universal circulation. Care must, however, be taken to dispose of any in one's possession before one crosses the Border, as they are not legal tender in this part of the kingdom, and it will be found a nuisance to get them changed.

A very excellent system is that of the Post Office Savings Bank. With a deposit placed there before one leaves home, and with one's bankbook in one's possession, one can withdraw any sum of money in any part of the kingdom at a couple of days' notice. More than thirty pounds cannot, however, be deposited during the year, and the whole sum to a depositor's credit is not allowed to exceed £150. It is therefore only useful in case of requiring small sums.

'TRAVELLING ACROSS THE Black Sea and the Caucasus from Constantinople, I arrived at Moscow in November, 1890. Anyone who has been travelling through a strange country for two or three days without stopping ... will easily understand my feelings of relief when I was told that the next station was Moscow, especially if my reader is tall, and has experienced that awkward position of being cramped for a long time in a railway carriage. The train stopped; and having collected my many wraps, I got out and at once confronted a true Muscovite winter, which my English clothing, notwithstanding the above mentioned rugs, was ill-fitted to face ... Because I stayed at an hotel some people became suspicious, and looked at me askance. On arriving in Moscow, many of the

English residents spontaneously opened their doors to me, and seemed to take great interest in my work. But one day, an article appeared in a London journal containing a reference to me and written by a well meaning but unwise friend; and then, laughable as it may seem, I was suspected of being a political spy. It was no laughing matter, however to me, for friends began to keep aloof, and I became uncomfortably conscious of being decidedly under a cloud. It was not pleasant either to drive about in a little open sledge in a temperature about 20 degrees below zero, the wind and snow driving full in one's face with clothes (except a shouba lent by a kind friend) only suitable for an English climate.'

Kate Marsden,
from On Sledge and Horseback to the Siberian Lepers, 1893

Mountain-climbing.

One of the most delightful amusements of the tourist, it should yet be indulged in with prudence, and undertaken with proper precaution.

If one is not used to steep ascents, or is out of practice with mountaineering, one must begin one's climbing by degrees. Nothing is so likely to injure from over-exertion, or to bring on heart and other organic troubles, as incautious over-exertion and violent fatigue

in climbing when one is out of training.

Begin, then, very slowly, without undue haste; and attempt at first nothing but what is well within your powers, no matter how ardent of spirits you may be. Breathlessness, or rapid beating of the heart, are signs, that you are doing too much; and they should never be disregarded.

Whenever these warnings occur, stop at once to rest

and recover breath; then proceed again.

In regions where there are elements of actual danger in mountain-climbing, to the stranger who is unfamiliar with the locality—as is the case in many parts of the Scotch Highlands, and in certain places in Wales, and among the hills of the Lake district—it is mere foolhardiness to refuse the services of a guide, who is even more necessary to lady tourists than to adventurers of the stronger sex.

Of course all hill localities are subject to mists, which form always a certain element of bewilderment; and in early spring or late autumn there is always danger of a sudden snow-storm, which has often terrible effects. It is never wise when in a strange part of the country to trust to one's own weather wisdom, and even one's own reading of the signs of the barometer may fail. Local lore is generally to be depended on, and should always be consulted as to the weather prospects of the day before one ventures on an expedition.

Should, after all these precautions, a sudden mist catch one unaware, it is useless to try and fight against it. All signs fail in an experience of this sort, and its very nature is so bewildering that it is quite hopeless to try and grope one's way. Any such endeavour will probably end in your getting further and further from the spot at which you are hoping to arrive, and may bring you into a position of extreme peril. The only plan is to sit down, and wait with as much patience as you can command till the mist clears, which it is pretty sure to do in the course of an hour or two, perhaps sooner. These mists are generally bitterly cold, with a piercing damp, which seems to penetrate to your very bones. For this, and other reasons, it is always well to carry with one an extra wrap—a warm light plaid, for preference.

Have your gown tailor-made, or, if you prefer to patronise a dressmaker, as plain in cut and finish as possible, and be particular not to let the skirts be made heavier than can be helped. This is a fault to which tailors are prone; probably the mind masculine is unable to grasp the fact that a woman cannot take active exercise in heavy garments.

Let the skirts be as short as possible—to clear the ankles. Nothing else is permissible for mountain work, where one must face bogs, deep heather, thorny gorse, and must not stumble into the hem of one's garments on the face of a rocky precipice. I must, however, draw the line at the modern feminine costume for mountaineering and deer-stalking, where the skirt is a mere polite apology—an inch or two below the knee, and the result hardly consistent with a high ideal of womanhood.

On the other hand, nothing looks more pronouncedly vulgar than an attempt to retain the fashionable dress of the town in the solemn majesty of the eternal hills, before whose presence all the light fripperies of folly and effect seem to die into impertinent flippancy.

You had better provide yourself with a good luncheon on mountaineering expeditions. The air has a peculiarly sharpening effect on the appetite, to which the exhilaration of climbing only lends a sharper edge; and the total impossibility of procuring other food than what one carries with one on the top of a lofty mountain peak is painfully borne in upon one if one's provision has not been sufficiently ample.

Hard boiled eggs are an excellent institution for mountaineering; but don't forget the salt and pepper! Sandwiches are also good; and, in Scotland, nothing surpasses a wheaten 'bap' cut open and spread inside with butter and honey. A small bottle of milk, or a flask of claret and water, will be found most grateful. Climbing is terribly provoc-ative of thirst; and it is fatal to drink of the mountain streams, clear and bright as they may be.

A stick is an indispensable addition to one's mountain-eering outfit. In some parts of Wales, you can get long stout staves for climbing, fitted with a strong sharp spike on the end, in the style of an alpenstock. This is by far the best sort of stick for the hills, and will help one over difficulties which nothing else will enable one to surmount.

A small compass should always be carried; and will be found of the greatest value in tracing one's way. Take your bearings before starting in the morning, and you will at least have some approximate idea of the direction in which you must steer your return journey. Mountaineering is very confusing work. Hills are so much alike in their main features, and change their characteristics with such extraordinary celerity as one changes one's point of view. Distance, also, is a peculiarly delusive thing in mountain districts.

A certain point may appear quite close, which, as you make your way towards it, recedes into space in a way which rouses your suspicions of witchcraft. For this reason you may find yourself a good deal further from home than you had any idea of.

To the woman who counts the highest happiness in life that which is attained by achieving a greater display than her neighbours, or in out-dressing a rival, there can, naturally, be little to attract in this form of enjoyment; but to a lover of nature, a true disciple of the picturesque and the beautiful, there is a charm and a fascination about mountain climbing that must be felt to be appreciated.

One is so exposed to the wind and the sun on mountain-tops that the effect on a delicate skin is often such as to burn and tan the face to a painful degree. A simple and homely remedy, which may be obtained in the most out-of-the-world localities, is sour milk applied thickly at night, and washed off with plenty of soap in the morning.

Night journeys.

Generally characterised with far more discomfort and fatigue than a journey by day, since many people find it impossible to sleep, and there is always a certain element of misery in a sleeping berth on a car, or on board a steamer.

The night trains to the North are furnished with sleeping cars, in which a berth may be obtained by an advance on a first-class fare; but for the second and third classes there is nothing for it but to make oneself as comfortable as circumstances admit.

Fortunate is she who can secure the whole side of a carriage to herself, of whatever class! This is not always possible, especially in the season, when the trains are crowded, and though I have always found the men in a carriage willing to put themselves to any inconvenience to accommodate a lady, still, with the regulation number on each side, one can only try to catch fitful dozes sitting up in utter wretchedness, and nearly breaking one's neck at intervals.

With a side, or even half a side, to oneself, one can manage far better. A cushion or two is a necessity, and rugs cannot be too abundant. A night in a railway carriage, even at midsummer, is a remarkably chilly affair, and the cold and piercing breath which comes just before the dawn makes one thankful for every available bit of extra covering.

The hat, or bonnet, must come off, and a fleecy wrap take its place. Stretched at length upon the seat, or even propped in the corner, with one's feet up, one may obtain some really good sleep, though the jar and noise of the train, the feeble shelter of the windows by the blinds and curtains, and the stoppages at various stations, all make it an affair of broken rest. At the large stations where one halts for one's morning meal, there are excellent and extensive lavatories, fitted with hot and cold water. You should always have, in your dressing or hand-bag, a clean soft towel, a brush and comb, and a piece of soap. Your toilet performed, you will find yourself so refreshed as to contemplate breakfast without the sense of absolute loathing with which it had inspired you before.

It is better, if you are not tired of the carriage, to have your breakfast brought to you there, rather than struggle for it in the noise and bustle of the refreshment room, where the smell of hot meat may not improbably deprive you of whatever appetite water and soap have summoned to your aid.

Packing.

There are some people so curiously constituted as actually to enjoy this ghastly preparation for a journey, but to the general public it is a sort of nightmare, a realisation of those hideous dreams, when one is for ever starting on a journey, and for ever discovering, at the very last available second, that all one's most cherished possessions have been left out of the trunks, which have been carefully locked and strapped, and are ready for instant departure.

Certainly some people possess a positive talent for packing, an instinct for finding out the precise corners fitted to contain certain articles, an inspiration in the matter of folding, compressing and arranging. I boast a female relation who is famous for her skill in this particular line. She was once going to America, and had herself performed the office of packing all her boxes, as she had at various times packed those of members of her family starting for all quarters of the globe. The Customs House officer—that dreaded functionary on the Atlantic voyage—boarded the vessel and began his search. When he opened the lid of the first box belonging to this particular lady he paused in admiration, and bowing respectfully to her, returned her her keys with the flattering remark, 'I really cannot have the heart, madam, to disturb such a beautifully-packed trunk!'

It is a mistake to let a maid do your packing, unless it is your own woman, who understands your particular fads, or you direct her in all her undertakings, which is quite as much a nuisance as doing it oneself.

As a first step in packing, have all your boxes brought and placed in the room where they are to be filled, as a guide to the amount of space which is available. Next, collect all your belongings which are to be packed in the same room. Put your linen in one place together, your gowns in another, and go over in your mind every accessory which accompanies each toilet, that you may be sure of forgetting nothing. When everything is collected, it is time to begin operations.

The stouter portmanteaux or boxes should contain the linen and heavier articles, the dress-hampers being reserved for gowns and lighter articles of dress only. The bottom of a box should be filled with the heaviest of its contents, the lighter ones being at the top. Linen should be rolled, each piece by itself, and packed together as closely as possible. It will crush less than in any other way, and take up far less room.

Books, boots and shoes, etc., should be packed with it, as heavy articles. Each pair of shoes, boots and slippers should be provided with a bag of its own, made of Holland linen bound round neatly with braid. A monogram or initials worked upon it adds to the effect.

Gowns are the terrible part of packing. Do what one will, in the present reign of dainty draperies and fragile trimmings, it is almost a physical impossibility to prevent crushing, and an evening gown can never make a day's journey in a trunk and retain its first freshness. Each dress should have a tray to itself, which should be furnished with tapes on each side to tie the skirt into place and hold it there. The folding of gowns is an art in itself, and can only be learnt in its higher branches from a lady's maid of experience. Mere words will not describe it.

Englishwomen do not understand the secret of the liberal use of tissue-paper as it is practised by their French sisters. Every fold of a really good dress should have paper placed between it, while puffed draperies, sleeves, etc., should be filled with crumpled rolls of the same, which keep them in shape, and altogether prevent creasing.

Laces, ribbons, etc., should be packed in small, light, separate boxes, and placed in the upper trays. Delicate, artificial flowers or daintily-constructed bows of ribbon had better be removed from hats or bonnets and packed in the same way, since the least crushing will damage their freshness, and that is their chief charm.

Be sure as you pack that you are putting in all that you are likely to require, and are not leaving out all your most indispensable possessions. It's an awful thing to begin dressing for a ball on your arrival at a house, and to find you have forgotten the only pair of slippers which will possibly go with your dress; or to have a whole costume spoiled by the dash of colour which was to have been imparted by a bright handkerchief or a knot of ribbon.

Packing for a return home is not half such a bother or a worry. You know just what things must go without the trouble of selection, and you also know that the going is a necessity, and that if they refuse to accommodate themselves to the limited space of the boxes, force may legitimately be employed.

'MEANWHILE, NO ONE had ascertained what had caused the heavy smash at the outset, and certain timid persons, in the idea that a hole had been knocked in the ship's side, were in continual apprehension that she would fill and sink … Below, in addition to the close over-powering odour of cabins without any ventilation, the smell of bilge-water was sufficient in itself to produce nausea. The dark den called the ladies' cabin, which was by no means clean, was the sleeping abode of twelve people in various stages of discomfort, and two babies. I spent a very comfortless four hours, and went on deck at dawn to find a thick fog, a heavy rain, the boards swimming with soot and water, and one man cowering at the wheel. Most of the gentlemen, induced by the discomfort to be early risers, came up before we reached Bedeque, in oilskin caps, coats and leggings, wearing that expression on their physiognomies peculiar to Anglo-Saxons in the rain.'

Isabella Lucy Bird, from The Englishwoman in America (written anonymously), 1856

Porters.

As I have already stated elsewhere, the duties of the porter in connection with passengers are somewhat limited according to the strict letter, though they are called upon to perform the most extraordinary and alien offices at times, and, being one of the most obliging classes of men in existence, they generally fill the situation admirably.

Arrived at the station, a porter is at the door of your cab or carriage ready to take your small parcels while you alight. He lifts down your luggage, deposits it on his truck, and wheels it away to be labelled.

He is called upon to give information as to trains, times, charges, and a hundred other subjects. At your request he will find you a seat in a good carriage, and place your hand luggage in the rack; then he retires with your boxes, deposits them in the proper van, and returns to tell you where they are to be found.

As the train arrives in a big junction or terminus a horde of porters stand ready to receive it. One makes for each carriage, and if you are lucky enough to be near the door, and are the first among your fellow-passengers to catch his eye, his services are yours. Should some luckier person secure him first, you may either ask him to call another porter for you, or else perform that office for yourself with the first disengaged one you can find.

At the small stations the supply of porters is very limited, and I have often wondered at the patience and good temper of one of these officials, attacked by half-a-dozen sets of people all at once, all clamouring for his attention and their luggage.

Your luggage secured, your porter will call you a cab, or find your carriage, and convey your luggage to it, or to the cloak-room, as you prefer. He tells the cabman or coachman the address, and then vanishes, having produced upon your mind the effect of one of the genii of the Arabian Nights—a slave of your lamp or ring.

During a journey a porter will fetch you a cup of tea, or a dinner from the refreshment-room, papers and books from the book-stall, refill your foot-warmer, and perform a hundred other services at your request. As I mentioned before, these are quite outside his province, and may justly be considered to entitle him to a recognition of his attentions.

Porters are, as a rule, specially kind and civil to

ladies travelling alone; in fact, they are, as a class, deserving of the highest praise, and a surly or disobliging member of the race is an experience so unusual as to excite one's profound surprise, considering how trying their daily work must be to body, mind, and temper.

Like all their fellow-creatures, porters are keenly sensible to kindness, and a pleasant word and hearty thanks for a little extra attention on their part are civilities which are seldom thrown away.

Pullman cars.

Known in America as drawing-room cars, were introduced from that country to this some years ago.

They are to be found upon all the long-distance lines, and are by far the most comfortable style of day travelling for the ordinary first-class passenger, being fitted up with every comfort and convenience.

For ladies making the long journeys alone by day there is no better method of railway travelling. There is every facility for seeing the country, as well as for travelling without undue fatigue and discomfort; and the ease of motion, especially on the smoothly-running express trains, contrasts delightfully with the rattle and jar so often felt on some of our inferior lines.

Railways.

The network of lines which intersects the entire country renders it easy for a traveller to get to any point by rail. There is, however, very often a lack of accommodation among rival lines, which is rather trying to their victim.

For instance, it is not one of the most delightful things in life to arrive at a junction at which your time-table has led you to believe that you will find a train waiting to take you on to your destination, only to behold the departing smoke of that train, as it whistles triumphantly out of one end of the station as you enter the other.

Also, it is very little balm to your feelings to be informed that the two companies have quarrelled, and make a point of upsetting each other's arrangements, and that your next chance of proceeding another stage in your day's journey will not occur for a couple of hours.

On some of these junctions, also, the porters of one line avoid having to convey passengers' luggage to the rival platform, so that there is small prospect of your getting it into another train, unless you can capture a porter belonging to the other faction, or are prepared to wheel it over yourself.

Generally, rival competition has an excellent effect upon the general improvement of a line and the excellence of its arrangements, and those lines which are most devoid of modern reform are those which enjoy a monopoly of traffic. Nowhere, perhaps, is more evident the short-sighted policy of lack of improvement and rational reform than on these railways.

Their miserable accommodation and high rates keep their traffic low, while on those lines where the rates are reasonable and the accommodation really admirable, the rush of passenger traffic is enormous, and the returns proportionate.

Railway keys.

Very useful articles to accompany one in one's wanderings. They are so constructed as to open the locks of carriage-doors on all lines of railway, and are portable, and easily carried in one's hand- or dressing-bag.

It is often the case that a porter cannot be found at a small station, or where a long train stops some of its carriages at the end of a platform, and one is a prisoner, in spite of all one's efforts to alight. Where the pause at the station is of limited duration every minute is of value, and one grudges the necessary waiting for someone to come and release one. With a key one is quite independent, and can enter or leave the carriage at will. These keys can be obtained at the book-stalls of stations at the cost of a few pence, and it is odd that so few people appear to avail themselves of them.

The return end [of one's ticket] should be carefully put by in a safe division of one's purse till the time that its services are required. It is a little awkward to arrive at the station on one's return journey, and remember that one has securely packed one's ticket away in the depths of one's biggest trunk.

Riding tours.

One of the most delightful forms of touring, to those who are fond of horse-exercise, and can afford the amusement.

Sometimes a lady goes alone on one of these expeditions with her husband or father, unattended by a groom, and relying solely on the ostlers at the various inns at which they intend to stop; but the attendance of a groom is far more comfortable in every way, and he can carry a convenient amount of luggage.

Heavy luggage, as in cycle and driving touring, must be sent on from point to point; but the actual immediate necessities must be carried with one. Of course, for one or two ladies starting on a riding tour alone, a groom is an absolute indispensable.

No lady should attempt a riding tour unless she is a really good horsewoman, and accustomed to spend days in the saddle. Other-

wise, she will find such an expedition fraught with difficulty, and even danger.

A horse should never be taken for a tour of this kind to which its rider is not perfectly accustomed. Many unusual conditions may arise to try both its nerves and its temper, and the rider should know perfectly with what description of animal she has to deal if she would have her tour one of enjoyment.

Notice should, as far as possible, be sent on to the inns and hotels on the route, engaging rooms and stabling. This will prevent a great deal of trouble and inconvenience. A tall hat will be found neither so comfortable or so suitable as a low-crowned felt one. A silk handkerchief for the neck may be carried in the pocket of the saddle.

Given fine weather, an agreeable companion, and a route full of picturesque and varied scenery, and the woman who loves her horse and feels herself never more at home than in the saddle, will find herself in the possession of a wealth of enjoyment which none but those who have experienced it can even begin to appreciate.

Stiffness at the end of a day's riding should at once be treated with a bath as hot as can be taken, followed by a quick and brisk rubbing in of Thilum or Hippacea, and the result will be surprising.

A waterproof cape should be carried to shield the shoulders in case of heavy showers, since it must be remembered that the habit is the one garment for the time being, and one does not want it wet through more frequently than can be reasonably avoided.

Sandwich-boxes.

By far the best means of carrying sandwiches with one. Shut up in a tightly-fitting box from the air, they keep fresh far longer, and the bread does not get stale and dry.

Sandwich-boxes are of every style, from the gorgeous silver article, engraved with crest and monogram, to the humble one of japanned tin, which, however, serves its purpose equally as well. I have found the latter sort answer thoroughly in keeping its contents in an excellent state of preservation. More than once, after a journey lasting from twenty-four to thirty-six hours, I have found some sandwiches, left and forgotten in their box, as good as when they were placed there. If they are so arranged as to completely fill the space destined for them, there is less chance of their drying. The box should, as far as possible, be kept cool.

Sea-bathing.

There are few things more invigorating and delightful than this pastime, while, at the same time, none should be indulged in with more prudence and caution. It is no uncommon thing to find people doing themselves real harm by what ought to be only a means of enjoyment and benefit.

Of the thousands who flock every season to the hundreds of sea-bathing resorts about the coast, there are really comparatively few who really understand the rules by which their indulgence in the pastime should be regulated.

It is, indeed, far safer never to take to a course of sea-bathing without medical advice; since, while to some constitutions it is harmful at all times, and in all places, to others it may be absolutely fatal under certain conditions.

For the strong and vigorous there is no time for a plunge in the sea like that of first rising in the morning. Being the time of day at which the majority of people are accustomed to a cold tub, there is far less shock to the system than later on in the day. There is also an invigorating effect in a bath in the sea before breakfast which one finds at no other hour, though the time one spends in the water should be short. A few brisk plunges are quite enough; a long swim will probably produce lassitude and weariness for the rest of the day.

It is also, by far, the most convenient hour for one's bath. A hasty toilette is admissible, and one's hair need not be carefully arranged before venturing down to one's machine. The bother of undressing and dressing again in the middle of the morning altogether deters many women from sea-bathing.

In bathing before breakfast it is wise to take one's morning cup of tea or glass of milk, together with a biscuit or a slice of bread and butter, before starting out.

Undressing should always be performed rapidly, to avoid getting chilled before one enters the water. This should be done briskly—by diving, if one can swim; if not, by a dash at once into the water, not a gradual descent. The head should at once be put under water, else headache and other ill results will be found to follow.

The time spent in the water should be devoted to swimming or active exercise. Standing still or dawdling about is both foolish and pernicious. Never stay longer in the water than common-sense dictates. Fatigue or chilliness should be a signal for coming out at once.

On leaving the water rapid friction should restore the circulation before dressing, which should be done as quickly as possible.

Bathing by machine is by far the most convenient form of dressing and undressing for one's bath. Some of these machines at certain seaside places are very comfortably fitted up, and are furnished with conveniences in the way of looking-glasses, shelves, hooks, and pincushions. Those are particularly nice which have a little outside apartment, with a slatted floor, where one may remove and leave one's wet bathing-dress.

Bathing from a house or tent has its drawbacks, as the run over the sands to and from one's bath is not comfortable. A bucket of water should be at hand to dip one's feet into after the return journey. Bathing from a tent has an additional disadvantage from the many draughts in which such an apartment abounds. Still, in small and remote places, unblessed by either bathing-machines or houses, tents are a real boon.

Bathing-dresses in this country have at last attained to the decorum and suitability so long absent from them, though possessed by most other nations. We are more seldom appalled now-a-days by the spectacle of a group of women attired in a loose blue serge garment de-

void of form or shape, and producing an effect upon which one would prefer not to dwell.

~~~~

One's hair is a great source of annoyance in sea-bathing. If it is tightly twisted up in a towel, having first been wrung out the moment one emerges from the water, it will generally be dry enough, when one has finished dressing, to hang over one's shoulders till the drying operation is quite finished. It is very bad for it to be put up while in any degree damp. Salt water has such an unpleasant effect upon the human hair, which it renders sticky, harsh, and disagreeable to the touch, that some ladies make a point of having theirs washed out in fresh water directly after having been in the sea.

This, however, entails a waste of a terrible amount of time if one bathes daily, as drying after fresh water takes far longer than after salt, and one cannot spend one's days after the fashion of a mermaid on a rock.

After a course of sea-bathing it is a good plan to have the hair well washed with the yolk of an egg, which should afterwards be thoroughly well rinsed out in clear tepid water. Avoid hot water, which will cook the egg, with most unpleasing results.

In America, as on the Continent, ladies and gentlemen bathe together—a plan which, once one is accustomed to it, strikes one as somewhat more sensible, and a good deal more decorous than our own method, as managed at most watering-places.

'**WE HAVE NOT** seen much of Melbourne yet, as there has been a great deal to do in looking after the luggage, and at first one is capable of nothing but a delightful idleness. The keenest enjoyment is a fresh water bath, and next to that is the new and agreeable luxury of the ample space for dressing, and then it is so pleasant to suffer no anxiety as to the brushes and combs tumbling about. I should think that even the vainest woman in the world would find her toilet and its duties a daily trouble and a sorrow at sea, on account of the unsteadiness of all things. The next delight is standing at the window, and seeing horses, and trees, and dogs—in fact "all the treasures of the land"; as for flowers—beautiful as they are at all times—you cannot learn to appreciate them enough until you have been deprived of them for two months.'

Lady *Mary Anne* Barker,
from *Station Life in New Zealand*, 1870

Soiled linen bags.

One of the most disagreeable things to have to carry about with one on one's travels is soiled linen, and one is only too glad to find any way of lessening the disagreeability. Perhaps the most satisfactory plan is that of the soiled linen bag, which, though it forms an extra package, is a great convenience in other ways.

Messrs. Barrett & Sons have some capital specimens of this kind of bag, made in extra stout brown canvas on a strong iron frame, and furnished with a good lock and two leather straps and handles. They form a bit of luggage which is by no means unsightly, and the possession of which is a source of endless comfort to the traveller.

Soiled linen may be stowed away in these convenient receptacles while one is stationary at any place, and either carried with one on one's travels or sent back to the laundress from various points upon one's journey.

Summer travelling.

In some ways summer is by far the most enjoyable season of the year for the pleasures of travelling, and possesses fewer drawbacks than other times of the year. Nothing in this world, however, is quite perfect, and there are certain drawbacks which are peculiar to travel at this 'sunny time of the year'.

First of all comes the heat, which is, to many people, a far more trying affliction than the most Arctic cold.

In some summer journeys it is impossible to escape this trial, though coach or steamboat travelling is a sufficiently cool exercise for a sultry day in July, even if the crowded space of a railway carriage presents less hope of alleviation. Still, even there, the rapid motion through the air imparts a certain breeziness which one might be unable to discover seated under the shadiest of trees in a leafy garden.

As antidotes to the heat, one can only suggest that the summer travelling gown should be made of the thinnest possible material which is consistent with the necessary stability of texture; that as few under-garments should be worn as possible; that a fan and eau-de-Cologne should be carried; and that all such heat-provoking causes as hurry, anxiety, and fretting should be religiously avoided.

Dust is another of the drawbacks in summer travel—one, perhaps, of which we do not often taste the full woes in this land of constant downpours. A dust-cloak is an immense comfort in the cases in which it can be worn. It is really frightful to contemplate the amount of dust one's garments are capable of acquiring and retaining, and the only hope is to cover them up as much as possible from the penetrating evil.

Flying particles of dust are very liable to get into one's eyes and down one's throat, causing great irritation and annoyance. A few drops of pure glycerine, swallowed slowly, have often a very-good effect in soothing the cough which so often follows on this tickling of the membrane, while the best remedy for a grain of dust in the eye is to plunge the face bodily into a basin of tepid water, and open the eyelids wide for a second or two.

I have often wondered that the most certain and speedy cure for the suffering and annoyance caused by the presence of a foreign body in that delicate organ, the eye, should be almost entirely unknown in this country. I mean the so-called eye-stone, the use of which is in common custom in America, and has been so for many years. This eye-stone is really the bone of a fish, found, I believe, on either the West Indian or South American coasts, and possesses extraordinary powers which appear to be quite unique. In shape it is somewhat like an opal—oblong rather than round, with one side flat, and the other of a slight convex. It is about the size of a child's smallest finger-nail, and of a yellowish white colour.

The eye-stone is slightly moistened, the lower eyelid drawn a little down, and it is inserted within. Almost immediately it begins to work its way slowly round the eyeball, and never stops till it has made the complete circuit of the eye, when it drops out, bringing with it whatever object of an alien nature it has encountered on its journey. The application of the eye-stone is perfectly harmless, painless, and devoid even of discomfort, and I have never known it to fail of achieving a perfect result if it was in good condition. An eye-stone may be used again and again, and may retain its properties for years, though I have sometimes known them suddenly and mysteriously lose all power.

To ascertain whether they are still efficacious, the eye-stones should be placed in a saucer and covered with vinegar. If they are good, they will begin to move about in the acid as if they were endowed with animation. Should they remain without motion, they have lost all virtue and are useless.

Thirst is another accompaniment to summer travel. As a general rule, it is better to bear it with what philosophy one can, since an endeavour to quench it often results in making it considerably worse. The milk which is now sold in most large stations at the various windows of the train is very refreshing, and generally of an excellent quality. Soda and milk form a very cool and pleasant beverage.

Stations.

These are of such a varied character, from the vast dome of a London terminus, looking like a city in itself, with its hotel, stalls, and bustling crowds, to the almost bare shed on some remote country line, that it is difficult to include them under one descriptive head.

There is a characteristic, however, which all railway stations appear to possess in common—I mean that of extreme ugliness. According to Mr. Ruskin,

this is perfectly correct and proper; usefulness being the only beauty of a railway or its accessories, and any attempt to soften down the natural repulsiveness of aspect which follows being a vulgar incongruity.

All the same, it seems as if there might be some attempt made to remove, at least, a little of the bald unattractiveness which strikes a chill of depression to the soul of the traveller, no matter how much use and repeated suffering has taught her the lesson of experience. There is a shuddering desire to escape from them as soon as possible—a nightmare association of leave-takings and missing luggage, a weight of bewildered noise and bustle and clamour which makes even the most ardent and devoted traveller only tolerate the station for what it represents.

Sometimes one comes upon a country wayside place where an attempt has been made to defy Mr. Ruskin, and the effect of a blaze of nasturtiums in a disused siding, or of neatly-laid-out flower-beds beside the platform is certainly such as to make one deride his counsels.

The station being merely the point of arrival and departure, generally a cave of the winds in winter, and a sort of young furnace in hot weather, it would be out of place to dwell at length upon the subject.

Tea.

Fortunately, this everyday article is not so rare a thing to obtain good of its kind in this country as in many others. Still, there is often a total incapacity on the part of the ordinary lodging-house and other domestic to fathom the idea that the achieving of good tea depends largely upon the fact of the kettle boiling at the time when it is made, not merely having boiled; and it is often more satisfactory to manufacture the article in question for oneself than to leave it to the tender mercies of the ignorant and incapable.

'The cup which cheers' is so great a factor in the comfort of the lives of many women of the present day, that it deserves special notice in a work devoted to the details of feminine travel.

Tea at the refreshment-rooms of railway stations and on board steam-boats

is often a mere parody on the real article—a fearful decoction which appears capable of performing a principal part in the historical episode of Queen Eleanor and Fair Rosamund, and of which one hesitates to partake, lest it should have speedily fatal results.

It is wonderful that so really simple and easy an act as the proper making of tea should be so frequently a perfectly unknown art. There are two or three principles whose practice alone is needed to ensure a result which is all that one could wish.

First, the water must not be too hard, and it must really be boiling. Secondly, the teapot must be well scalded, before the tea leaves are placed in it, and the boiling water poured upon them. And thirdly, and lastly, the tea must be allowed to draw just long enough to be strong, and not long enough to acquire the bitter flavour of the tannin.

In travelling it is as well to take with one one's own tea. You will by this means ensure a better article in all probability, and one often gets accustomed to a special flavour, and prefers it to any other. With a home-comfort, or an etna, one can be perfectly independent, and provide tea for oneself at any hour of the day or night. A capital little arrangement is a perforated cup of bright metal, with a cover, which fits upon an ordinary teacup. The tea is placed in this receptacle, and the water poured upon it. A few minutes suffice for the drawing, and then the tea-maker, with the used leaves, is bodily lifted out, and a capital cup of tea remains.

Milk is the great difficulty in travelling tea-making. It cannot always be easily obtained, and milk carried about with one in a bottle does not long retain its freshness in hot weather. Some people do not object to the condensed or Swiss milk one buys in small tins. It has the advantage of being extremely portable, but I must confess, personally, to finding its effect detestable in tea or coffee.

For those who fancy the Russian plan of a slice of lemon as a substitute, there is a great comfort in being able to dismiss the milk problem altogether from one's mind. The lemon is easily carried, does not lose its freshness, and is really far more refreshing in its effects.

I must not conclude without quoting a remark once made to a friend of mine by a celebrated London physician, whose treatment of the nervous diseases of women has made his fame world-wide. 'I ought not say a word against tea,' he said, 'since it sends me most of my patients.'

There cannot be a doubt that the intemperate use of this most delightful and refreshing beverage is becoming a grave evil amongst Englishwomen. From the washwoman, who keeps her tea-pot on the hob, and takes the contents, like Sarah Gamp, 'when she is so dispoged', to the fashionable woman, who indulges in the same luxury six or seven times a day, from her early tea till the last cup which awaits her in her dressing-room on her return from the evening's round of amusements, there is probably too much tea drunk, and with too little discrimination.

Over-strong tea acts as a powerful stimulant, but it has the worst possible effect upon the digestion and the nerves; and constantly repeated doses injure without producing any other effect. It is a thousand pities to abuse by excess one of the most rational, pleasant, and innocent indulgences which are open to the use of womankind.

Tea-pots.

As I just now observed, tea on one's journey is too often a ghastly experience: therefore it is an excellent plan to carry made-tea with one, not only on one's travels, but on picnics, and other excursions of the same sort. This can be managed by means of one of the so-called Russian or Singapore teapots—a basket lined with thick wadded stuff inside, in which a tall china teapot rests, with its spout projecting through a small aperture left for the purpose.

Tea in one of these pots can be kept hot for many hours, and as the tightly-fitting lid is furnished with metal handles, it can be conveniently carried about. The tea is made first in another teapot, and then poured off into this receptacle, in which, as it does not also contain the leaves, it is in no danger of becoming bitter from overdrawing, however long a time it may be kept there.

Toilet requisites.

Soap should always be carried with one on a journey. Pears' soap, the world renowned, is perhaps the best toilet article manufactured, but there is a bath soap which possesses, in my eyes, a superior excellence. This is Samphire soap, which forms a particularly rich lather, and gives a softness and smoothness of effect which is simply delightful.

Soap should be carried in one of the little metal boxes specially destined for the purpose, which keeps it in excellent preservation.

A little washing soda or oatmeal is useful in softening hard water. Frizzetta is a wonderful preparation by which, if it be used to moisten the hair before curling, an extraordinary effect is produced in 'keeping in' the curl. It has been tried in ball-rooms, at sea, and on the dampest days, with success; and for a lady traveller will be found a most valuable possession.

Many ladies are very subject to chapped faces and hands in travelling in sun or wind; and the chapped lips from which many of them suffer are a real source of discomfort and annoyance. Pure glycerine is about the best and pleasantest cure for this. It should be well rubbed in, regardless of the smarting which may at first ensue. In the case of chapped hands, they should be washed first, and not quite dried, when the glycerine is applied. After it is thoroughly rubbed in, the superfluous stickiness should be removed with a soft towel, and a pair of old gloves should be worn. This remedy is best applied at night.

A good toilet water is often desired by ladies in travelling, and is also most useful to add to water. A few drops in one's basin are a great refreshment when one is hot and travel-stained. Florida water is an excellent preparation of this sort. It is not expensive, it is very cooling and refreshing in its properties, and it contains nothing which can be harmful to even the most delicate skin. Lavender water is a great favourite with many people, and is also useful in the same way; though it does not, with any justice, represent the delicious fragrance of the plant whose name it bears.

Trunks.

These form an important item of luggage, and must be considered by themselves. As a general rule, the fewer trunks and boxes one has the better in every way. It is a frightful nuisance to have a lot of boxes to look after in travelling, and one or two large ones are decidedly better than a whole pile of small ones.

Time was when a lady's trunk, to be large, must also be ponderously heavy. As a nation, we are rather given to fancying that anything meant to last must needs be of vast weight, and that solidity and strength must necessarily go hand in hand.

Of late years we have learnt wisdom, and have discovered that it is possible to manufacture articles which shall be light, durable, and strong; lady's luggage has certainly been one of the chief

gainers by this national discovery.

Tin or steel trunks have always the name of lasting longer than any other, but I have not myself found this borne out by practical experience.

They are very apt to dent with the rough usage of travel, and I have known their arched tops to be bent in and broken by a heavy weight placed on them in the luggage-van. Then, too, the paint or japanning scratches and peels off, and the exterior soon becomes a sorry spectacle. Dents in the side, too, make it almost impossible to get the trays either out or in; and altogether, for wear, appearance, and general utility, I should never advise a trunk of this description.

It is a comfort to those lady travellers whose sense of the artistic and the beautiful used to be shocked by the quaint conception of painting and graining a tin trunk to bear a ghastly air of simulating wood, that these articles are now generally painted and enamelled in pretty and subdued colours, and no longer attempt their melancholy bits of deception, which had about the same effect upon the mind of the beholder as a juvenile wig above a wrinkled and faded face.

French trunks are light, commodious, and, though very ugly, are convenient and not ruinously expensive. They are waterproof, fitted with light trays, generally furnished with divisions for special articles, and may be had in grey and various dark colours.

Perhaps the best box ever invented for a lady's use is the Saratoga trunk. It was so-called, as most people know, from the fashionable American watering-place of that name, where ladies are wont to resort with wardrobes of so lavish and extravagant a description that a special build of commodious, yet light, trunks was invented for their accommodation.

The larger-sized ones are seldom seen in this country, being, in truth, so enormous that the mind of an ordinary hostess would quail at the spectacle of a fair guest arriving with four or five of these ark-like pieces of luggage—a moderate amount for a fashionable American girl to have in her train.

Indeed, two porters on an English railway would probably think themselves necessary to lift one of these big trunks, which a negro waiter in a Transatlantic hotel will fling over his shoulder and carry upstairs at a run.

One admirable accessory of the Saratoga trunk was, I believe, first introduced into this country by its means. This is the castor-fitting to the bottom of the box, by which it can easily be moved about in a room, instead of being dragged and pulled, to the detriment of itself and the carpet. These castors or rollers are set in the wooden bands under the bottom, so that the weight of the trunk does not rest on them injuriously.

Mr. J. Allen has a very neat and convenient little article called the Ladies' Utilis, or short journey trunk. It is small, light, and portable, about two feet and a-half long by fourteen inches high and wide, and has five compartments—for a dress, a bonnet, linen, light articles, and boots.

This is a capital little trunk for taking on journeys of a few days, and, indeed, will contain a tourist's requisites for a far longer time.

It is a great comfort that mere travelling entails so much less luggage than visiting, and that one may make a long tour in comfort with far fewer belongings than would be needful in a visit of a couple of days to a friend's house.

A most capital idea has been patented by Messrs. Drew and Son, whereby their convenient ball-dress trunk can be turned into a hanging-cupboard when its destination is reached. This consists of a row of portable hooks, which can be fixed at one end of the trunk inside. It is then stood on end, and the dress-skirts, which the box is long enough to contain without folding, are hung up within. The whole forms a most neat and effective wardrobe, and will be greatly appreciated by ladies who know the effect produced upon crushable gowns by being left to lie one upon another for any length of time.

Before starting on a journey it is as well to thoroughly overhaul all one's trunks to ascertain if they are in thorough repair as to locks, straps, etc., etc. The inner bands of webbing, which hold up the lid, will often be found to be showing signs of wear or coming loose, and should be carefully attended to at once, on the good old principle of the stitch in time saving nine. Nothing is so likely to injure a trunk as a defect in these little securities. If they give way, the lid will fall back, and probably break its hinges.

It is better to make all one's umbrellas, parasols, sticks, etc., into one parcel which will bear one's address, and be less likely to be overlooked than a single loose article carried in the hand.

Unpacking.

Never an operation to be so much dreaded as that of packing, since it is always easier to pull to pieces than to build. The easiest system upon which to conduct it is that of putting every article into its destined place as it is removed from the box which has contained it. This is easy enough on one's return home after an absence, when one knows just the proper nooks and corners where all one's belongings are accustomed to live; but when one has arrived at a strange place, things are somewhat different.

Even on visits when one certainly looks for a fair accommodation for one's property, it is not always forth-coming, and I have sometimes been rather appalled in houses where one would certainly think one had a right to expect better things, to find the chest of drawers and the wardrobe in the room assigned to me filled to overflowing with the gowns and garments of the members of the house, with not so much as a spare inch left for the needs of the unhappy guest. This is, of course, utterly inexcusable, and should never be allowed to occur.

with the laws of gravitation, all the things one wants most and oftenest invariably find their way to the bottom), such a bother, I repeat, is far beyond the first trouble of removal and putting away.

If the space for stowing away is ample, unpack most of your belongings. It seems a simple matter at first, to leave a good many of them where they are, and a considerable lightening to the labours of unpacking, but it is not so in the end. Things left in one's boxes are apt to get tossed over in a hasty search for a missing article, and the bother of going to the very bottom of a trunk half a dozen times a day (by a curious provision of nature, no doubt connected

It is just as well to carry with you some large sheets of fine yellowish-brown paper, to line the drawers and wardrobes with which you are accommodated on your travels. They will take up little room, and can be carried off with you when you go, to serve for the next occasion. It is true that one will generally find these receptacles already neatly papered, but in nine cases out of ten the paper has been left there after the former occupants of the room; and there is some-

thing not particularly tempting in the idea of placing one's possessions in a place where one does not know what has preceded them.

Begin by lifting out the trays, and putting them on one side. You can then remove the heavy articles from the bottom of the trunk; or, in the case of gowns, the ones least likely to crush, which, of course, you have had the prudence to place in the lowest part. These will again be placed in the lower parts of the drawers, or on the least eligible hooks in the wardrobe, so that the same conditions with regard to them can be observed.

Articles of one sort should all be placed together. For instance, if the exigencies of packing have forced you to scatter your linen broadcast through half your trunks, you will now collect it together in one drawer, and not allow it to stray away into several. Nothing facilitates a quick discovery of a needed article like having it in the company of its fellows.

In unpacking on arriving late at one's destination, the first objects of consideration will be the articles required for one's toilet, and for the night. It is wise, therefore, always to place these articles together, and where they can be easily reached. It is a trying experience to have to pursue a truant dressing-slipper or hairbrush through half-a-dozen packages, especially when one is at the last stage of fatigue and sleepiness.

To turn out all one's possessions in admired confusion over bed, chairs, sofa and other articles of furniture, before proceeding to find a place for the reception of anything, is a very favourite system with some impatient members of my sex, who will, however, find by experience that they have saved themselves neither time nor trouble by this apparently simple process. It is an old rule that a little expenditure of pain at the beginning saves a large outlay of the same article later on, and in nothing does this hold good more than in the undertaking of unpacking.

The time spent in carefully disposing of one's belongings is not wasted, and there is a vast amount of comfort in having, according to old-fashioned proverbial philosophy, 'a place for everything, and everything in its place.'

'ON OUR WAY, we neared some junks lying in the river, that had come from Siam and Cochin-China; the mast of one of them had been scathed by lightening; and the people were offering sacrifices and giving thanks to their gods for their deliverance from death. The gentleman went on board, and distributed tracts, and copies of the Testament. Then we passed on, about four miles down the river, and turned into a creek, where was a pleasant landing-place. There we walked up a hill, and came to a farm house; it was a mere shed, but there was a poor woman there who understood the rites of hospitality. There was something in her manner particularly attractive, because her politeness seemed to proceed from real kindness of heart. While we were partaking of her good tea, a crowd of people came to look at us. My costume especially attracted their attention, and I took off my bonnet, and allowed them to see the style in which my hair was dressed; I was quite willing to gratify their curiosity, as they seemed very respectful.'

Eliza Jane Bridgman, from Daughters of China, 1853

Waiting-rooms.

These places of public accommodation, whether provided for passengers by steamer, rail, coach, or any other mode of conveyance, are, as a rule, apartments of desolation, and surrounded by every association of gloom.

Waiting is not a pastime to most of us, and the mere fact of these places being connected with that weary period before the starting upon a journey would be sufficient to cast a cer-

tain amount of melancholy about even the brightest apartment.

But waiting-rooms, as constituted by the powers of travel in this country, leave no room for the impressions of mere sentiment, but force their ghastly realities upon one with a brutal violence. Apparently, mortification of the flesh and spirit are two objects held firmly in view by the projectors and carriers-out of the scheme of waiting-rooms; and the suffering traveller is fain to admit that their efforts have been crowned with a perfectly satisfactory success.

Abroad one often finds waiting-rooms which are in charming contrast to what our national idea appears firmly to have grasped as the correct thing, and I shall never forget the comfort and pleasure of waiting a couple of hours at the Mayence station, where the fittings and decoration of the first-class waiting-room are those of a salon, and the low, deep easy-chairs were a positive boon and refreshment to aching and travel-worn limbs.

Over the ladies' waiting-room presides its attendant guardian, the woman in charge. She is supposed to attend to their personal wants, and expects a fee of a copper, even if the regulations of the company do not exact this toll. She will take charge of wraps, small parcels, etc., for which she is responsible while they are under her care. For a longer period, or for one's heavy luggage, there is the cloak-room, where all articles may be deposited on paying a small fee for each package.

The waiting-room woman will fetch you tea or other refreshments from the refreshment-room, if you request her to do so, and will also render you other small services. She is generally a downcast and saddened personage, no doubt reduced to a state of mild melancholia by long years spent in the joy-destroying atmosphere of her surroundings.

Walking tours.

To anyone who is fond of walking, strong and healthy, and a lover of nature, a pedestrian tour offers tremendous attractions. Every year ladies appear to take up this special form of amusement with more energy, and the more its advantages of easy management, inexpensiveness and enjoyment become known, the more popular it will probably be.

It is absurd on the part of most women to undertake a daily average of distance, such as would form the ordinary allowance of a man on an expedition of the same sort, and many a woman has become an invalid for life, and prevented other women's rational enjoyment of a healthful and delightful pastime, because she was deaf to the voice of common sense, and insisted on attempting walks which were far beyond her strength.

Begin by walking short distances daily, and stopping to rest when you are fatigued. You will soon be able to increase your daily allowance, and at last achieve with ease what would at first have been an absolute impossibility.

Prepare beforehand for a tour by getting well into training, and by accustoming yourself to the conditions under which the tour will have to be made. Plan out your route beforehand, as far as may be possible, and set down as the allowance of probable distance for each day something under the amount you believe yourself capable of managing with ease.

Ten miles a day is a respectable allowance for a lady pedestrian, carrying a certain amount of her own luggage; and a great deal of ground can be covered in merely a ten days' tour of the sort.

On no account, however, should you set out on a walking tour in new shoes, or in ones which have not become perfectly easy and comfortable by use. If they are at all stiff they should be worn for some days previous to starting, that they may become easy to the feet before the continued test of a walking tour is brought to bear on them. It is positive torture to walk in shoes which are uncomfortable, and from the friction and fatigue to the feet produced by a walking tour there is special reason to guard against this source of inconvenience.

Luggage must consist mainly of what can be carried in the knapsack on one's back, and must be reduced, therefore, to the least possible proportions. The nightdress should be of the finest cambric—it will take up less room.

Choose a brush and comb of small size, and make all your toilet arrangements with a view to the economy of space. One item is indispensable, a pair of thin slippers. If you can stand them without heels, they will take up the less room, and if they are old and loose, they will be the greater comfort.

A pair of thin stockings—silk for choice—should accompany these slippers; and you cannot realise, till you have tried it, the rest and refreshment of changing for these your dusty and way-worn shoes and stockings.

A stick is a great comfort on a walking tour, and helps you over the last few miles of the day in a really wonderful way. As, however, one should be provided with an umbrella, and it is not possible to carry both, it is a good plan to provide oneself with an en-tout-cas with a handle stout enough to serve the purpose of a staff.

A waterproof is a necessity; but as even every added ounce is a grave matter when one is one's own beast of burden, it should be of the lightest possible make. One of those American gauze waterproofs is the best—not a mackintosh. These are as light as a feather, yet quite shower-proof, and when rolled up and carried either above or below the knapsack add but little to its weight.

A good road map is needful; and it is as well also to

obtain detailed information about the day's route before you start out on your journey each morning. It is not safe to trust to wayside information on the subject; and it is a very poor amusement to wander three or four miles out of one's way.

For a walking tour, it is best to choose a part of the country where the roads are good, and the scenery of a varied and pleasing character. Long monotonous stretches of level highway have a tendency to damp one's ardour, and to make one cast a regretful thought to swifter modes of locomotion than that provided for us by nature.

Watering places.

A subject of really grave importance in travelling, where soiled linen, never a very agreeable thing at any time, becomes a positive bugbear when one has to drag it about with one on one's wanderings.

Fortunately, laundry work is so quickly done now-a-days, that in most places where one stops over a couple of days, one can send a reasonable amount of linen to the wash one morning, and get it back again the next night, so that there is no actual necessity of burdening oneself with it in an unwashed condition. The people at your hotel

or lodging will recommend a laundress, and tell her to call for your things, which you should have ready, with a list of the articles, clearly and legibly made out, to accompany them.

On the return of the goods the washwoman will expect payment, of course; and bills of this sort should never be allowed to run on, even if you are remaining for any length of time in the place; since these poor people live in a hand-to-mouth manner, and are dependent for their daily food upon the

payment they receive for their work.

~

For articles torn or lost in the wash, the laundress is responsible, and payment for her washing should be withheld until she restores the missing article, or makes it good. As far as garments can be used which do not require washing, it is as well to indulge in them. For instance, a petticoat of black or grey alpaca is an excellent substitute for one of a material which will readily soil and require doing up.

Things washed in a hurry are often insufficiently aired, and care should be taken not to put on one's clean linen while it may still be damp. In winter, when a fire is at hand, the linen should be placed before it to thoroughly warm before being used or put away. In summer merely to hang it up in the air, and, if possible, the sun, will be found sufficient to air it perfectly.

~

By the sea there is endless pleasure and interest in studying the 'common objects of the sea-shore', and the little pools left by the ebbing tide contain a mine of wealth to her who will take the trouble to investigate their mysterious recesses. Collecting seaweeds, or materials for an aquarium, will supply one with occupation and amusement during a long stretch of idle time. Sketching is an endless resource, but, of course, it is not everyone who possesses the needful talent for its achievement.

~

Winter travelling.

To some people the pleasures of winter travel outbalance those of summer. These are generally people of robust constitutions and strong frames, who do not mind a little 'roughing it', and who collapse under the enervating influence of summer heat.

To the majority of people, travelling in winter, in England at least, is not a thing of unmixed joy; and all one's ingenuity is brought to bear upon the subject of how best its drawbacks may be mitigated. Our system of railway accommodation is one by no means suited to the extremes of climate, and while our small compartments are stuffy, ill-ventilated, and broilingly hot in summer, they are too limited in space to allow of any means of heating them in winter; and so constructed that it is almost a physical impossibility to escape draughts.

I have dwelt so much and so strongly upon the importance of warm wraps, that it will hardly be necessary for me to repeat that an ample supply of these luxuries is a most important provision for travel in cold weather. Hot bottles and foot-warmers have also been held up to the notice of my readers, and I may add that a very delightful addition to one's comfort on a journey in cold weather is the little hand-warmer of electro, filled with hot water, which may be carried inside the muff, and keeps one deliciously warm.

It is an excellent rule to start warm on a journey, one is far more likely to keep so. If one begins one's travels with cold feet and a chilled frame, one may not improbably continue in that condition to one's journey's end, or at least during a greater part of it. Of course, the great danger to health in travelling during the winter months is through colds and chills of all sorts, and these should be carefully guarded against.

It is wise when one starts on a long journey in a snowstorm to carry with one an extra allowance of provisions. The experiences of travellers during the last few winters, when trains have been buried in drifts of snow for hours, and even days, should make us prudent in this respect, when a provision of food may be of really inestimable value.

Foreign
Travel.

Continental travel.

The whole conditions of travel on the Continent are so essentially different from those at home that they require a portion of space specially devoted to them. From the first moment when the traveller sets foot upon foreign soil, and sees the strange surroundings, the quaint dresses, and curious habits of the natives, enhanced by the clear air and brilliant sunshine, so different from the softened atmosphere at home, she experiences all the effect of having entered into a new life. The sounds are equally novel—the foreign tongue, the eager excited voices, the constant clangour of the bells, the street cries, and the calls of the workpeople. She can hardly realise that it is really the self who left the shores of England but a few hours back.

The altered conditions of the simplest everyday acts of life—food, sleep, and such ordinary habits—must be rendered beneficial by adopting ways suited to the changed climate and country; the interests of travel must be allowed to have full sway.

The traveller who insists on living and eating as if she were still in England will find that habits which are best suited to the dull and depressing climate to which she is accustomed will not allow of continuation in the clearer, lighter air abroad, and, if persisted in, will cause general disorganisation to the whole system.

It is perfectly certain that the cultivated mind will derive infinitely more pleasure and benefit from Continental travel than that which is untrained.

To an imperfectly educated nature half the fascination and charm will be wanting, and it is such persons as these who are to be constantly heard declaring abroad that the life and manners of the Continent are intolerable, and nothing can begin to compare in qualities of every sort to what one finds in Great Britain. A certain degree of cultivation is probably needed even to show people the commonest beauties of nature, still more to make them in any degree appreciated. While it is only the cultivated mind, filled with knowledge of history, literature, and science, and trained to the right perception and enjoyment of the true and the beautiful in art and music, which can in any way enter into the understanding and delighting in the rich treasures of life upon the Continent.

The language is a certain stumbling-block to many people's enjoyment of foreign travel; and it certainly adds enormously to one's pleasure in sojourning in a strange land to be able to understand and to converse in the alien tongue of the inhabitants. But a really very scanty stock of French and German will suffice to carry you over the whole of the Continent in safety and comfort; while, if you confine yourself to the beaten track, and to hotels frequented by English and American travellers, your own language will be enough to trust to.

Luggage is a great trial in Continental travel. The amount allowed to each person is ridiculously small, according to our ideas, and every extra pound must be paid for at a rate which mounts up to a perfectly exorbitant sum when the weight of luggage is anything like what one would consider a fair allowance for one's needs at home. It is best, therefore, to compress one's belongings into as limited a space as possible, and to do without much which one would consider to be indispensable ordinarily, but without which one will find oneself quite able to get on when the need arises.

Washing is so well understood in most foreign countries that one's clothes will be the gainers by being submitted frequently to the ministrations of foreign laundresses; while, at the places frequented by travellers, these are so used to rapid operations that one can get one's linen washed

and done up in an incredibly short space of time. This does away with the necessity of carrying with one many changes, and is a great factor in reducing one's luggage to the requisite scanty dimensions.

Trains abroad travel, as a general rule, slower than our English ones, and while the stations at the large centres are replete with comfort in many cases, the ordinary run of these places by the way are devoid even of ordinary proper accommodation.

The train service is often very imperfect, and unless one travels first or second class, one can seldom find place on the quick trains, but has to jolt along from station to station at a rate which greatly increases the fatigue of the journey.

Money is a vast source of trouble, not only from the difficulty in understanding its correct value in an unfamiliar coinage, but also because of the different coinages into which one's money must be changed in travelling through several different countries. Formerly every little German state had its special coinage, and the effect was perfectly maddening to the uninitiated traveller; but this has fortunately been changed, and one can be at least secure of marks and pfennigs all through the empire.

Postage-stamps, however, still retain their individuality to a certain extent, and should always be invested in in small quantities, or else one will find oneself burdened with a supply of perfectly useless articles once one is over the border.

In changing money one always seems to be the loser. Of course, a certain commission is deducted, but besides that, the coinage of most countries but our own being decimal, it is exceedingly difficult to give an exact equivalent to the value of our £ s. d., and we are not the gainers in consequence.

It is necessary to be very careful where one has one's money changed, and unless one is quite certain of a money-changer, he may stoop to the traditional tricks of his trade, and make a considerable profit out of your ignorance.

Hotels abroad are, of course, of all kinds, and of every description. If you can afford to pay high prices, you may have the accommodation of a prince, while, where your charges are less, your accommodation, of course, keeps pace with the reduction.

The pension, or boarding-house system, is admirably understood and managed in most Continental countries, and is a very convenient, as well as a much less costly way of living than that afforded by hotels.

In many places abroad, too, especially in those towns most frequented by English visitors, there is an excellent system by which boarders are received into respectable private families, of a position and education which would, in this country, render an entry into their midst on such terms almost an impossibility.

English and American travellers are always supposed, abroad, to be rolling in money, and both able and willing to pay any price which may be asked them for any article whatever. Upon this supposition they are subject to the most outrageous demands; and, unless they are old and experienced travellers, are generally cheated on all sides. It is well, if possible, to ascertain the real and legitimate charge for services and accommodation, as well as to have some general idea of the value of articles in the shops. This point once ascertained, stick to it with all the firmness of which you are capable, and refuse to add a farthing to what you offer. You will al-most invariably gain your point in the end.

Passports have of late years fallen into such disuse that they are not necessary in most of the best travelled parts of the Continent. It is, however, often a great convenience to have this means of identification in case of tiresome contingencies arising; and quite recently, since the relations between certain Continental powers have become strained, considerable trouble has been caused by an absence of passport. It is, therefore, safer to be provided with this security, even if it should not be called into requisition.

Duties are very often a source of annoyance to those travellers who have not sufficiently acquainted themselves beforehand with the Customs regulations of the various countries through which they are to travel. These vary to a considerable extent—tea is contraband in most Continental countries, and only a very limited amount is permitted to be carried over the frontier. In other countries all articles of food fall under the same ban, and I actually have known a stick of chocolate seized at the Swiss frontier while its owner was in the act of beginning to eat it.

All articles must be removed from the carriage and the luggage-van, and carried to the building where the inspection is made. You are asked by an official whether you have anything to declare, and your answer in the negative is generally sufficient, though, if he insists upon searching your luggage to verify your assertion, you will have no right to remonstrate, as he is not exceeding the bounds of his duty. You must undo all fastenings from your luggage, and place it open for inspection. This accomplished, the official has a perfect right to leave your possessions scattered broadcast, and to decline to restore them to their places, though, if you are civil, and have given him no cause for suspicion, he will generally be ready to make things pleasant.

It should be borne in mind that he is but a public servant, acting under rules and regulations which bind him as much as yourself, and that civility and courteous readiness on your part to assist his performance of his duties will probably bring about pleasant treatment at his hands.

The difference in food is one which at first is apt to strike the stranger with a feeling of dislike, and the many courses of small dishes appear unsatisfying and meagre to an appetite used to joints and plain puddings. It is, however, a far more suitable method for the requirements of the climate, and the obdurate Briton who insists on retaining her native bill of fare under conditions so different from those at home, will probably regret before long having done so.

'OUR PERSONAL OUTFIT consisted, in addition to a few changes of woollen underclothing, in a guanaco-fur mantle, a rug or two, and sheath-knife and revolver; besides, of course, the guns and rifles we had brought for sporting purposes. The cartridges for the latter, of which we had a great number, formed the heaviest item of weight; but notwithstanding the care we had used in our calculations, so as not to take more provisions than we wanted, the goodly pile which formed when all our luggage was heaped together was rather alarming, and we found that at least twelve horses would be required to carry it. Fortunately we were able to procure three mules, who, between them, carried more than six horses could have done, without, moreover, suffering half as much as the latter condition from fatigue, or the severe heat which we occasionally encountered.'

Lady Florence Caroline Dixie, from Across Patagonia, 1880

Sea-voyages.

So very much of the subject of foreign travel to dwellers on an island must consist of a consideration of travel by sea, that perhaps no more fitting conclusion could be made to a work of this description than that which is furnished by the treatment of voyages.

the whole subject is one which must come under the practical experience of the lady traveller who leaves her own shores; and to anyone who has never made a journey by sea the idea is often fraught with difficulties which will be found only to exist in the imagination.

From the short passage across the Channel to the voyages of our mail steamers to India and Australia,

Many ladies dread the very thought of a sea-voyage, not only on account of the expected horrors of sea-sickness, but because of the perils they will have to encounter, which appear terrible in their inexperienced eyes. In point of fact, that feeling is generally soon lost on once finding oneself on board. The vast steamers which convey their passengers as in a kind of floating hotel, are certainly calculated to inspire confidence in the heart of even the most timid, and once one has fairly started upon one's voyage, the ship seems so entirely a little world of one's own, that one loses the sense of its being a mere frail fragment at the mercy of mountainous billows and ferocious gales.

Indeed, though of course sea-voyages have their element of danger, like every other form of travel, there is no doubt that these are often greatly magnified by the terrors of imagination, and many a nervous individual has suffered the agonies of death by shipwreck, merely at the sound of the sailors' tramping feet overhead, or the boatswain's pipe of all hands on deck to shorten sail.

One timid lady, on a particularly prosperous voyage to Gibraltar, was so overcome with terror at the usual heavy roll in the Bay of Biscay that she dressed completely, and sat all night in her cabin prepared for instant death; but adorned with all her most valuable possessions in the faint hope of rescue from a watery grave. She was afterwards heard to complain bitterly of the reckless conduct of the young men on board, whom she could hear singing comic songs in the saloon outside, when every minute might be their last!

On board the troopships dinner-dress is a necessity; and, indeed, on most sea-voyages a certain amount of change of costume is expected for the evening. If the voyage is into warmer latitudes, thinner clothing must, of course, be also taken with one.

No washing can be done on board ship, so a sufficient supply of linen must be taken to serve for one's needs while one is afloat. If old linen is taken, which can be thrown overboard when done with, it will be found a great addition to one's comfort, and prevent a most disagreeable accumulation of soiled articles during one's residence on board the ship.

All toilet requisites should be kept close at hand, and where they can easily be reached. To have to hunt for these necessary articles while the ship is rolling so that one can scarcely stand upright, and when one is perhaps feeling desperately ill, is an experience from which those who have once tried it are apt to shrink.

The most useful arrangements for this purpose are the so-called cabin-bags, which can be obtained from the outfitters, or made at home at an outlay of a shilling or two. They are best and neatest made of brown Holland linen, bound with scarlet braid, and consist of a flat piece of material, fitted with numerous pockets, and furnished with loops of the material to contain such small toilet articles as nail and tooth brushes, etc., etc. A watch-pocket and a

pincushion form very useful additions to this convenience, in the pockets of which are placed one's night and toilet requisites, book, pocket-handkerchief, flask of eau-de-Cologne, etc., etc.

A deck chair is a most necessary addition to passengers' luggage on a long voyage, since there are no such conveniences provided among the ship's accommodation, and the sitting upon deck in the fresh air and bright sunshine forms one of the pleasantest elements of one's whole life on board. Deck chairs are of various sorts, from the elaborate and most deliciously comfortable cane lounge fitted with arm-rests, special places to hold one's book, glass, etc., on which one may recline luxuriously, to the humble folding carpet chair, which is convenient

from its portability.

Care should be taken in selecting a deck chair not to get one which is too light, otherwise your enjoyable after-dinner nap on deck may be abruptly terminated by a sudden lurch of the vessel, and you may find yourself overturned, chair and all, and sent flying to the other side of the ship in a manner more sudden than graceful.

Time on board is counted by bells, not clocks; and it is somewhat confusing, at first, till one learns that these bells are but eight, and stand as well for the half as the whole hours; and that when they have rung their full number, they begin and repeat their performance over again from the first, and so on through the day and night.

One of the great peculiarities of life on board is the sharing of one's cabin with total strangers. It is a curious experience at first to find oneself in the company of a number of women one has never seen before, and thrown into close contact of association with them for a longer or shorter period of time.

It is a common saying that it is the passengers who make a pleasant voyage, and this is in no case more true than of one's fellow cabin-passengers. Individual characteristics come out in a more marked way under such circumstances than in perhaps any others; and one has every chance of judging of the various forms human nature can assume.

The subject of sea-sickness, that bane of the traveller by sea, has been dealt with elsewhere. These must, however, vary much with different constitutions; and the real remedy for this trouble has never yet been discovered. Perhaps keeping one's berth, and remaining perfectly still and quiet, is about the best way of keeping the enemy at bay, but even this will by no means always suffice to achieve it. Food on board ship should be taken often, and sparingly at a time. Meals will be brought you on deck by a steward in reasonable weather, if you wish it; and to remain as much as possible in the fresh air is one of the wisest possible means of preventing an attack of the dreaded affliction.

A doctor is carried on all ships making long voyages, and his services are at the disposal of the passengers, should need arise for them, though it is unfair to expect that he will be able to do much towards removing the commonest form of suffering at sea.

Amusements of all sorts take place on a voyage of moderate length—ship quoits and shuffle-board by day, and amateur theatricals, concerts, and dances to enliven the evenings. Service is held on board on Sunday by a chaplain, if one is present, or, in the absence of any clerical element, by the captain.

Now-a-days, when the increased facilities of communication, and the greater freedom of transit, have placed distant lands within easy reach of our own, and made travelling everywhere an infinitely simpler and more pleasant thing than

it once was, lady travellers have vastly multiplied in number.

Even in the most remote parts of the world, where, a generation ago, they would not have ventured, ladies now travel in perfect security and with every advantage.

Miss Gordon-Gumming, Lady Brassey, and Miss Bird are among some of the most famous names of modern travel; and hundreds more whose names are never even heard of, outside their own particular circle of friends, have made journeys almost as wonderful, and as full of interest.

Continental travel has been so thrown open to women, that it is the most ordinary of experiences now to find abroad ladies travelling alone, or in parties of twos and threes, and the sight is too common even to excite remark.

Emancipated womanhood is a term too often of ridicule and reproach, and—alas! that it should be said—is not always undeservedly so. Women may abuse the privileges too long withheld from them, in the first bewilderment of feeling a new power in their hands. But none, perhaps, is less open to abuse, and surely none is more excellent in itself and its results, than the power which has become the right of every woman who has the means to achieve it— of becoming in her own unescorted and independent person, a lady traveller.

To many, the power thus obtained fails to bring with it the pleasure it would otherwise bestow; since lack of experience or ignorance of the comforts and conveniences so indispensable to the real enjoyment of travelling form an actual drawback to their thorough appreciation of its joys and benefits. To such persons the experience of others may be a great help, and save them from many disagreeable bars to the full pleasure of their journeyings at home and abroad.

It is said that experience is the best teacher: it might justly have been remarked, more emphatically, that it is the only teacher whose lessons are worth anything. It is, however, not only one's own personal experience which is to be trusted.

Much can be learned from the experience of others, and in a way which possesses a peculiar satisfaction, since the price we pay for it is far less costly.

It is, as I have said before, in the hopes of helping those members of my own sex to whom the world of travel is still a wide and unexplored region, and before whom its perils and its discomforts loom with a totally unnecessary dread, that this little book has been written.

My one desire has been to offer hints and suggestions which may smooth some of those difficulties which appal the novice in travelling from her path.

If, by my endeavours, I have in any way assisted my sisters in their wanderings, or encouraged a single woman to join the path of travellers by land or sea, I shall feel that I have achieved the object of my labours, and that my task has, indeed, not been in vain.

The End